THE

Portable
Baker

THE

Portable
Baker

BAKING ON BOAT AND TRAIL

JEAN AND
SAMUEL SPANGENBERG

RAGGED MOUNTAIN PRESS
CAMDEN MAINE

International Marine/
Ragged Mountain Press

A Division of The **McGraw-Hill** Companies

4 6 8 10 9 7 5 3

Copyright © 1997 Ragged Mountain Press

Library of Congress Cataloging-in-Publication Data

Spangenberg, Jean.
    The portable baker : baking on boat and trail / Jean and Samuel Spangenberg.
        p.   cm.
    Includes index.
    ISBN 0-07-059871-1 (alk. paper)
    1. Baking.   2. Outdoor cookery—Equipment and supplies.   3. Cookery, Marine—Equipment and supplies.   I. Spangenberg, Samuel.   II. Title.
TX763.S63   1997
641.7'1—dc20   96-23357
                                      CIP

Questions regarding the content of this book should be addressed to:
Ragged Mountain Press
P.O. Box 220
Camden, ME 04843

Questions regarding the ordering of this book should be addressed to:
The McGraw-Hill Companies
Customer Service Department
P.O. Box 547
Blacklick, OH 43004
Retail customers: 1-800-262-4729
Bookstores: 1-800-722-4726

A portion of the profits from the sale of each Ragged Mountain Press book is donated to an environmental cause.

The Portable Baker is printed on 55 pound Sebago, an acid-free paper.

The Portable Baker was typeset in Adobe Garamond and BureauGrot

Printed by R. R. Donnelley, Crawfordsville, IN
Design by Eugenie S. Delaney
Production by Janet Robbins and Mary Ann Hensel

DEDICATION

To our children, Laura and Ward, our families
(Bell, Padfield, Shirreffs, and Spangenberg),
and our friends. Intrepid taste-testers all,
and constant wells of inspiration,
encouragement, and support.

CONTENTS

PREFACE

⟜≡⟩

I n the ten or so years that I've been developing recipes for
Adventure Foods, I've had many pleasant opportunities to talk
to boaters, kayakers, hikers, speed hikers, expeditionists, skiers,
RVers, Boy Scouts, Girl Scouts, campers, and just about any other
outdoor sportsperson you can think of.

When a device from Strike 2 called the BakePacker first came on
the market sometime around 1989, it was the beginning of a whole
new era in baking for the boat or the trail. Up until that time, if you
wanted baked items on your trip, you had the choice of the reflector
oven, the Dutch oven, the skillet, or baking on sticks and rocks. In
other words, the methods were time-consuming, the cooking accessories were heavy, and most consumed too much fuel to make baking practical as an everyday part of your outdoor experience.

Now, in the BakePacker's wake come Cascade's OutBack Oven,
the BushBaker, the GSI aluminum Dutch oven, Coleman's collaps-
ing oven, the Sportsman Oven, the Rome pie baker, the Rome
double-handle baker and griddle, the Burns-Milwaukee portable
Sun Oven, and numerous types of pressure cookers, to name a few.

For boaters, this offers the widest possible range of options to
fulfill the desire to bake. Hikers and campers have more limited
options because of the weight of the bakers or ovens and fuel,
since—unless they are car- or RV-camping—all of this must be
carried on their backs.

It has been my goal to introduce boaters and campers to a wide
variety of baking devices and options so that you may make a more
informed choice. But then, having made your choice, what good is
a baking device without great bread recipes? That's where this book
proves doubly helpful.

Whether you want to add bread to your menu to boost your
caloric intake, or simply to enjoy the taste of it, I think you will find
this book invaluable with its wide variety of quick breads, yeast
breads, flat bread, batter breads, sweet breads, cakes, and dessert bars.

I'm sure that boaters, without the weight restrictions that backpacking campers have, will be able to cook the yeast breads more
often than campers can. I also know that a dyed-in-the-wool baker
(that's Southern for someone who loves to bake) will practice his or
her art—and it is an art—no matter what the circumstances.

Finally, I'd advise you never to try a new recipe for the first time on the trail or on the water. Test it at home first. After high levels of physical activity, you don't have the time or energy to face a major flop. Do your homework first; it's part of good trip planning. That way, you'll feel comfortable with your procedure. And remember: All recipes are easier the second time around.

The recipes in *The Portable Baker* are from family and friends, the King Arthur Flour Company, Presto, The Society for Range Management, and White Lily—as well as myself. I have tried to give credit to material from other sources, and any omission is unintended.

Sam and I genuinely hope you enjoy the recipes I have included in this book. We also would like you to share with us your favorite recipes and baking tips; perhaps they could find their way into our next book. You can write to us in care of Adventure Foods, 481 Banjo Lane, Whittier, NC 28789.

Happy baking and bon appetit!

Jean and Sam Spangenberg
February 1997

A Note on Recipes

❖ ❖ ❖

I've listed recipe ingredients in *The Portable Baker* in both conventional and dehydrated (dry) forms. The dry ingredients give you the option of mixing the recipe at home and packing it in a sealable bag for backpack or galley. You need only add water at the campsite or anchorage. These dry ingredients are available from any number of mail-order companies. For a list, see Appendix H, Sources, on page 160.

ACKNOWLEDGMENTS

Any publishing endeavor requires someone to believe in you and what you have to offer. Sam and I would like to thank the staff at Ragged Mountain Press, with special thanks to Jon Eaton and Tom McCarthy for all their assistance, encouragement, patience, and effort.

Numerous companies gave freely of their knowledge, time, experience, equipment, and recipes. Special thanks to:

Brinna Sands of King Arthur Flour Company, for her willingness to share her time, invaluable baking information, and wonderful recipes from King Arthur's *200th Anniversary Cookbook.*

Pamela Banks for her information and Banks Fry-Bake Oven.

Burns-Milwaukee Sun Oven Company for its information and assistance and the Real Goods Catalog for assisting my search for the solar oven company.

B West Outdoor Specialties for its Boma Cooker and Potjie Dutch oven.

Good Gear for the use of the BushBaker.

Glacial Stainless International for its willingness to help with information—and for the aluminum and cast-iron Dutch ovens.

Elizabeth Hand at ESHA Research for nutritional information.

Mark One Outdoor Outlet for its Coleman collapsible oven.

National Presto Industries for its kind help and willingness to share recipes from its *Official Presto Pressure Cooker Cookbook.*

Rome Industries for its information, pie iron, and double Dutch oven/griddle.

Charles "Bud" Rumburg at the Society for Range Management for his kind assistance with information and generosity in allowing reprints of recipes from *Trail Boss's Cowboy Cookbook.*

The Caferros at Strike 2 Industries for always being willing to assist with information. Denny Caferro was a friend and business associate and will be greatly missed by all who knew him.

The White Lily Flour Company for allowing us to reprint its recipe for Yogurt Batter Bread.

Special thanks also to the following good friends for their willingness to help, test recipes, read, edit, and listen: Tom Roderick, Sr., Thom Jaros, Bill Cook, Evie Barrett, Pat McCoy, Lisa Gravier Rhinehart, Janet Fong, Carol Brown, Betty Campbell, Melinda McWilliams, Joan Childers, Mike and Margaret Miller, Linda McAuliffe, Tom Roderick, Jr., Linda Kotika, and Hank Schuler.

* CHAPTER 1 *
The Baking Impulse

resh-baked bread! What can compete with the heady aroma of fresh-baked bread? It fills the air and excites your senses, making your mouth water and anxiously await your first bite of crusty warm bread.

As a child, I don't remember my mother making loaves of bread; but she made biscuits, and cornbread, and wonderful yeast rolls. Everyone loved it when my mother baked yeast rolls. I never ceased to be amazed at the variety of items that could be created from one basic dough: cinnamon buns, pecan twirls, doughnuts, and coffee cake, just to name a few.

One of the reasons that I'm still so fascinated by breads and baking is that there are still lots of new breads waiting to be created, by me or maybe you.

Don't Be Intimidated

My best advice, if you want to bake and have people raving about your breads and cooking, is to never let a recipe intimidate you.

I guess I am really a lazy cook. Don't tell Julia Child (whom I admire as an expert baker and cook), but I never sift my flour, salt, and baking powder or soda together before making a cake. Once you realize that sifted flour has more volume than unsifted flour, you can reduce the amount of flour required in recipes by about one and one-half tablespoons per cup (ten percent) and use unsifted flour. I have done this many times with great results.

I have also intentionally dumped all the ingredients in at the same time and beaten them all together. It did not affect the outcome of the recipes. If you are going to bake, on a boat or on the trail, you have to trust your own judgment about what needs to be done. It's quite simple: You will be there, and the cookbook author will not.

There are exceptions, however, recipes that really do require close attention to detail—for example, angel food cake, sponge cakes, or any other cake that requires the whites to be whipped separately or the yolks to be beaten until they've doubled in volume. I suggest you restrict this type of cake to your home-cooking adventures unless you have a huge galley or a well-equipped base camp for cooking.

Make and Remake

Not all of my culinary investigations or creations have met with success, but that's what keeps me interested. As I mentioned in my book *The BakePacker's Companion*, I often "remake" cakes or cookies. Usually the remade item is better than the original. Just as stuffing or dressing is made from precooked bread, or a mixture of bread and cornbread, other baked items can also be turned into new and delicious desserts. Bread pudding is an example of a remade food, using leftover biscuits or bread.

When I remake a cake or cookies, either because they didn't turn out the way I wanted them to, or because they weren't eaten before they got stale, I add about a cup of boiling water, and beat it back into a batter. I then add whatever I think was missing: oil, if it was too dry; sugar, if it wasn't sweet enough; or—if I'm turning it into cookies—extra shortening or oil and sugar. I think you get the idea. One thing you must do is add enough flour to make up for the water you have added, and baking powder or soda to make it rise again. If the cake was frosted, you may or may not need to add sugar. Have fun experimenting with a remake of your own items. Remember, you were going to throw this out anyway, so if you aren't happy with the results, toss it to the birds, or remake it yet again. I have found it helpful for outdoor cooking to make a small pancake to test the batter before cooking the whole batch.

The main idea of this type of cooking is using what you have. Aside from remade cakes and cookies, you can use your day-old bread or biscuits to thicken soups, stews, and fruit. Simply crumble them up and let them continue to air-dry. Store them until you need them, then just put the crumbs in until your dish is as thick as you want.

The whole idea of giving you the remade cake information is just to show you that recipes are only starting points, they are not commandments carved in stone. I believe that as soon as you realize this, cooking can become exciting.

Nutritional Information, Including Controlling Diabetes

Those of you who have flipped through this book have already noticed that there is more than a little nutritional information included with each recipe and in the appendices. I should like to spend a moment to tell you a bit about it.

In my own business I have found it necessary not only to create nutritious recipes for high activity levels but occasionally to tailor foods to meet the special nutritional needs, or biological intolerance, of my friends and customers. The Genesis R & D nutritional computer database program from ESHA Research has been absolutely essential in this work.

From the database I have generated two sets of essential information for each recipe: recipe totals and dietary exchanges. The recipe totals provide the basic information that people seek most often in retail product labeling. Do you need to increase your protein intake during competition sailing? The information is right there. Need to climb, or bike, or paddle all day? The carbohydrate content is right there. Trying to balance your protein, fat, and carbohydrate intakes to some specific level? Again the information is immediately available.

For those of you interested in determining the distribution of calories by percent, here is some helpful information:

Each gram of fat contains nine calories. Each gram of carbohydrate contains four calories, as does each gram of protein. Let's use the Beer Yeast Bread recipe on page 36 as an example. It has 2,138 total calories, with 58 grams of fat, 341 grams of carbohydrates, and 38 grams of protein. The total number of calories from fat for this recipe is 522 (58 × 9). With some quick arithmetic, you can determine that 21.4 percent of the Beer Yeast Bread's total calories come from fat (522÷2,138 × 100). Using the same process, we find that 63.7 percent of the Beer Yeast Bread's total calories come from carbohydrates (1,364÷2,138 × 100).

We have purposely not given the nutritional data based on per serving amounts. Serving sizes listed with recipes are just guidelines, and the true number of servings per recipe will depend on how large or small you make your biscuits or rolls and how thick you cut your bread.

Just remember that you must always divide the recipe's total nutritional data by the number of servings.

The second set of data, dietary exchanges, will be of particular interest to diabetics and those preparing food for diabetics. One of the earliest, non-invasive treatments of diabetes is to attempt to control caloric intake to avoid the need for more invasive therapies, such as oral or injected insulin. Careful and continuing use of the exchange values permits diabetics to calculate what food category to reduce if something else is eaten from another category. The information here can be lifesaving.

For non-diabetics the information that follows, as well as the exchanges themselves, should also prove instructive. The careful balance of food type intake for diabetics is not significantly different from the carefully balanced food intake (for control of carbohydrates) necessary for good health, exercise, and even professional competition.

There are about 16 million Americans with diabetes, but in 8 million people the disease has never been diagnosed. That means about one person in seventeen has diabetes—and half of them don't know it.

Food Exchange

Normally, food is converted first into glucose cells during digestion. Those cells are stored, or later transformed into immediate energy by the hormone insulin. Diabetics don't seem to have a problem turning the food into glucose, but production of insulin to convert the glucose to energy is a real problem. Some diabetics produce insulin, but it is ineffective. Others produce too little insulin. Still others produce no insulin at all. This lack of insulin is responsible for the continuing high blood-sugar levels characteristic of diabetics.

All diabetic problems call for careful control of glucose levels (through food selection and intake) and insulin levels (by introducing insulin to the body). Most diabetes control begins with the choice and amount of food eaten, because that can reduce the severity, or even the necessity, of insulin medication.

Food exchanges were developed to help diabetics maintain normal blood-sugar levels, thus avoiding hyperglycemia (high blood sugar), the potentially dangerous insulin reactions that might occur in attempting to reduce high sugar levels, and hypoglycemia (low blood sugar).

The diabetic uses the food exchanges to stay within a prescribed diet. Just as you and I might be told to eat only 1,500 calories a day, the diabetic might be told to eat three milk, four vegetable, four fruit, six bread, five lean meat, and seven fat.

Food exchanges are divided into six categories. The following chart gives you the nutritional values that make up one exchange in each category. For example, one fat exchange is five grams of fat and has 45 calories; whereas one milk exchange has 12 grams of carbohydrates and 8 grams of protein and no fat. If a diabetic chose to use one cup whole milk, which has fat, then he or she would be using not only a milk exchange, but 1½ fat exchanges as well.

The exchanges act as a careful balance of foods that give the diabetic 50 percent calories from carbohydrates, 20 percent from protein, and 30 percent from fat.

Category	Carbohydrates grams	Protein grams	Fat grams	Calories
Fat	0	0	5	45
Milk (skim)	12	8	0	80
Vegetables	5	2	0	25
Fruit	10	0	0	40
Bread	15	2	0	70
Meat				
lean	0	7	3	55
medium-fat	0	7	5	75
high-fat	0	7	8	100

Once a person has been tested and found to be diabetic, a doctor will prescribe a diet based on the food exchanges. This diet will be adjusted to stabilize the person's weight, based on individual metabolism and exercise levels. The new nutritional information on labels makes it easier for the diabetic to calculate food exchanges for any food item, but believe me, it takes practice to do it quickly.

Those of us who have suddenly noticed our arms are too short to read the newspaper, and that our family doctor doesn't look old enough to be one, should take the time to attend a diabetes screening (most diabetics go undetected far too long in this country). Then we should write to the American Diabetes Association for their free *Exchange Lists for Meal Planning*. If you have a friend who is a diabetic please pass on the address below.

I have given only basic general information regarding diabetes. If you need further information, contact the American Diabetes Association, Diabetes Information Service Center, 1660 Duke Street, Alexandria, VA 22314. Their toll-free telephone number is (800) 232-3472.

Boldly Go, Boldly Bake

Now you are asked to accept the challenge: Boldly go where few bakers have gone before (except, perhaps, on a chuck wagon or aboard the Federation Starship Voyager), into the woods, out on a boat, up in a plane, on the trail, or to the nearest, or farthest, camp site. Here's to becoming happy bakers wherever you may choose.

Bread's Early Beginnings

❖ ❖ ❖

Breadmaking is an ancient craft—Egyptians and Mesopo-tamians were known to be making bread at least five thousand years ago. The Bible indicates that there was leavened bread before the Hebrews' exodus from Egypt, and it says they fled before their bread had time to rise, so they had to eat unleavened bread or matzo.

Egyptians discovered that untended dough would begin to ferment after a few hours, forming gas bubbles in the dough that remained during the cooking process. The baked-in bubbles we know so well today made the bread softer, lighter, and more palatable.

The Egyptians may also have discovered that the froth from their beers and other fermenting beverages could make bread dough rise. In any case, they were well versed in the craft of breadmaking, and they continually developed better ovens in which to cook their bread more efficiently.

Paintings and hieroglyphics on tombs demonstrate that Egyptians took a keen interest in the growing and harvesting of grains and breadmaking. In fact, a loaf of bread 3,500 years old was found in one of the tombs—surprisingly well preserved, but probably the stalest bread in history.

But the Egyptians and Mesopotamians were not the first humans to bake bread. For example, we know that ten thousands years before the birth of Christ, Swiss lake dwellers were making some form of crude bread. Here are a few other significant dates in breadmaking history:

8,000 B.C. Women in the Near East were using sticks to dig holes in the ground and plant wild grass-seed. It was the beginning of agriculture and the end of the human hunter-gatherer era.

7,000 B.C. By now, humans were deliberately cultivating grains such as emmer wheat, barley, and millet.

4,000 B.C. Wheat crops were being grown under irrigation.

3,500 B.C. The invention of the plow, drawn by domesticated animals, vastly increased the amount of wheat and other grains available for bread.

100 B.C. By now, a hundred years before the birth of Christ, breadmaking had become a commercial industry. At this time, there were 258 bakeries in Rome alone.

During the reign of Roman Emperor Julius Caesar, bread flour was made available on a class basis. The kind of flour you received was determined by your social status. High-ranking people received white flour; the lower classes had to make do with coarse dark flour. The grades of flour and their dispersal were governed by law.

Caesar's regulations seem unfair to us now, but unintentionally (and ironically) he was doing the peasants a favor, because the coarser flours were healthier—much higher in fiber and nutrients.

During four hundred years of Roman rule, Britain became the granary of the Roman Empire. When the Romans left, they destroyed all they could, to negate Britain's agricultural advantage. But the Scandinavian and Saxon conquerors of Britain introduced a grain that had been a staple in their countries for centuries. That grain was rye, and it quickly became one of Britain's main cereal crops.

In Europe, the town baker enjoyed considerable standing in his community and people often took their own bread to him to be baked. But in America, bread baking among the immigrants started off as a home industry because settlements were not large enough to support a baker.

American "thirded bread," made from a mixture of wheat, rye, and Indian meal (cornmeal), was a variation on the mixture of wheat and rye flours known by the British lower classes as maslin. (Wealthy British ate only white bread, of course.) The thirded bread mixture has endured and remains popular even today as Boston Brown Bread.

These coarser breads were usually leavened by sourdough alone, but sometimes by sourdough used in conjunction with ale yeast. The brewing of ale and beer was the duty of the housewife, and explains the use of barm (ale or beer froth) in early yeast breads.

The colonists did their baking over an open fire, and it was backbreaking work indeed, but eventually the fireplace became common and it spurred the development of many innovative cooking devices. The swinging crane enabled the housewife to move large cauldrons of food toward or away from the fire. Footed pots allowed food to be cooked at the side of a fire, or over the embers, as did long-handled pans. French braising dishes featured an ingenious concave lid that held glowing coals or embers. Double-glazed earthenware dishes with tight-fitting lids could be buried in the hot ashes. Gradually, the process of cooking, and especially baking, became easier and more predictable.

In 1862, more than 150,000 settlers received land distributed under the new Homestead Act. Most often they had to cross hostile territory to reach their grants, so these early settlers took with them their hopes, their dreams, and a three-legged pot called a "Dutch oven" that had a concave, lipped lid. Dutch traders brought large quantities of these pots to exchange for other goods; and pretty soon, explorers, trappers, traders, and later cattlemen, came to depend upon the Dutch oven. In 1813, a used Dutch oven sold for four dollars—a week's wages.

✻ CHAPTER 2 ✻

Baking Equipment

*W*hen I first started thinking about doing a book about portable baking devices, I imagined there would be only a handful to consider. But as I started to list them, I was surprised at just how many options do exist for those of us who want a little more out of our cooking experiences while backpacking, boating, RVing, camping, and kayaking. I have tried to include all of the baking devices on the market. If I have excluded any, the omission was not intentional.

Food is a major part of the getaway experience. Food can salvage a bad trip, or at least make it more tolerable. If you add wonderful homemade bread to the equation, well, just the thought of fresh bread makes most people perk up. It's the ultimate comfort food. You only have to mention that it's made-from-scratch bread (no store mixes) and people start imagining they can smell it coming out of the oven. They can actually feel their teeth crunching into that crust.

I'd like your adventure baking experiences to be as successful as possible, but for that to happen you'll have to make some choices about the best baking device for your particular outdoor activity.

CHOOSING A BAKING DEVICE

The successful outdoor baking device for your activity should meet the following criteria to be a successful part of your gear.

1. Light enough for you to manage easily. For example, you wouldn't want to carry a cast-iron Dutch oven on your back for six weeks. But you might want to carry one if you were boating or camping in an RV.
2. Able to cook the types and quantities of breads you want to cook. For example, if you wanted crispy sourdough bread, you wouldn't take a pressure cooker to do the baking.
3. Easy to put together, clean up, and store conveniently.
4. Relatively simple to operate.
5. Compatible with your budget, considering the life of the baking device and its overall usefulness. For example, can you use it at home, too? Can it be used for more than just baking?

6. Able to work with your current heat source.
7. Safe to operate.

HINTS FOR SUCCESSFUL OUTDOOR BAKING

Once you have selected your baking device or devices (most outdoor folks wind up with several types for their varying needs), a few tips for making your outdoor baking easier and more successful might be in order. I suggest you review this list before each trip, until it is part of your planning routine.

1. Try the recipe at home first. You will have better success outdoors if you know how the recipe should turn out and the quantity it will produce. You can then adjust serving sizes. Remember, the serving sizes listed with the following recipes are just guidelines, and the true number of servings per recipe will depend on how large or small you make your biscuits or rolls, how thick you cut your bread, and so forth.
2. Regardless of the type of baking device you use, you'll find it more convenient to pre-mix all your dry ingredients in a plastic bag at home. Then label it well, or write your instructions on a slip of paper and place it, and the bag of mix, inside another plastic bag. If you are using dry yeast, you can blend it into the dry mix also.
3. Whether you are using baking powder, yeast, or sourdough, take along some extra baking powder that you have tried at home, just in case the yeast or sourdough doesn't rise. You can then work some baking powder into the bread dough and salvage it for dinner. It won't be exactly the same, but it will be fine for averting a breadless meal.
4. It's a good idea to carry one or two extra cups of flour in a plastic bag. For a start, it will come in handy for making drop biscuits. Make a simple dough, drop spoonfuls into the flour, and shape on the baking surface to eliminate the need to roll out rolls or biscuits. It will also come in handy for dusting your pastry cloth, for dusting your bread dough as you knead it, and for many other uses. Determine how much flour to take by how much and how often you plan to bake, then put an extra half-cup of flour in the baggie for each time you plan to bake on your trip. Remember you can always use the leftover flour for gravy, thickening, coating fresh fish, and so on.
5. If you're making pancakes, tortillas, or other fried breads, you can carry single-portion packs of mayonnaise to use for your

frying oil. Just squeeze the mayonnaise into the skillet or pan and it will melt back down to the oil. It will not give your food a mayonnaise flavor, and it is much easier to manage than a bottle of oil that might leak. Discard and pack out any unused portion of the packet; it won't keep.

6. Mark increments of measure on your drinking cup with a metal knife or carbide marking pen. That allows it to double as a measuring cup. Do the same thing to your spoon, for a measuring spoon.

7. Always check the water temperature carefully when using dry yeast. It should be only warm to the touch. If it feels hot to your finger or wrist, it will kill the yeast.

8. Never use warm or hot water with sourdough yeast. It will kill the yeast. Sourdough yeast requires cool water. But never use iced water as it will cause the yeast to become inactive or dormant. If the water feels just cool to the touch, it is fine.

9. Be aware that sometimes the amount of water in a recipe needs to be reduced or increased for your particular baking device. For example, the BakePacker requires twenty-five percent less water in bread mixes because the mixture is cooked inside a plastic bag, which limits evaporation. Mixtures baked in open pans may evaporate more.

10. Remember to divide the calories or diabetic exchanges by the number of servings you actually cut from the baked item. Servings and snack sizes will vary, depending on who divides them up, as will the calories and exchanges.

11. It is important to think carefully about what you'll need on an outdoor trip. You won't generally have the advantage of a convenient store to supplement your needs. You must take everything with you.

12. Planning for your food needs should not be less important than your selection of the appropriate clothing or shelter. They are all elements of your survival and should be planned as such.

13. No matter what type of baking device you use, always be careful and conscious of the possibility of a burn. Go prepared, taking a hot pad or oven glove along. It is also a good idea to carry along an aloe-based product or some form of burn preparation. I like Dr. Outdoors First Aid Jelly. It has an analgesic in an aloe base for topical relief. It is also good for sunburn.

14. Do not try to cook more than the recommended amounts in your baking device, regardless of the type you have chosen. It increases the cooking time of the item, tends to overheat, and decreases the efficiency of the oven.

15. Plastic bags are very handy for mixing dough. They keep less-than-sanitary hands off the mix, and eliminate the need for a bowl or pastry cloth. I like the gallon-size zip freezer bags.

16. The two-gallon size zip bag will even work for letting dough rise, if you insist on two rising periods. Otherwise put the dough right in the pan after you have mixed it in the bag.

17. You can also roll tortillas or pie crust inside the two-gallon-size zip bag. Just make sure you first dust it and the dough well with flour. After use, the bag can be folded away, flour and all, until the next time you need it.

18. Remember to pack all of your trash out with you. With care, our recreational country, on land or water, can last for many future generations. But unless each person makes a conscious effort, it will perish before our eyes.

I hope these tips will help you in your baking endeavors. If you have other tips that you feel should be included next time, please let me know. I welcome your help.

BAKING DEVICES YOU CAN BUY

The BakePacker

The BakePacker, made by Strike 2 Industries, is one of the simplest baking devices I've ever seen. It's basically a small grid of aluminum, encircled by a thin aluminum ring that is slightly taller than the grid. This exterior rim helps to keep the food directly over the grid for even

The standard (left) and ultralight BakePackers.

heat transfer, and has the side benefit of giving the bread or cake a nice round shape. The grid acts as a heat exchanger and evenly transfers the heat from boiling water to your foods by a method thermal engineers refer to as the "heat pipe phenomenon."

Because the heat is so evenly dispersed, the BakePacker allows you to bake bread, cake, or even an entree in a plastic bag. Yes, you read that right. I didn't believe it would work either, but I have used a BakePacker for seven years, and I can honestly say that it's the easiest and lightest baking device on the market today.

Since a good deal of the heat in the baking process removes moisture from the food (rather than in actual cooking), with the BakePacker you reduce the amount of water called for in a recipe by 25 to 30 percent to avoid producing a pudding-like texture.

To use the BakePacker:

- Put your dry mix in a plastic bag and add water.
- Squeeze the bag to blend the mix.
- Put one inch of water in your cook pot.
- Place the BakePacker in the pot.
- Set the bag of mix on the BakePacker, fold the top of the plastic bag down, and squeeze the mix out of the corners of the bag.
- Put the lid on your pot, and bring the water to a boil while you put up your tent, gather wood, or roll out your sleeping bag.

In fifteen to twenty-five minutes, depending upon the batter and your altitude, you can have pizza, chocolate cake, honey cornbread, and so forth. You can't burn or overcook your food as long as you have water in your pot—the temperature of boiling water is constant, regardless of the heat applied (though altitude will affect the temperature at which water boils). My favorite feature of the BakePacker is that there is no cleaning up afterward. You do need to pack the plastic bags out with you after they have been used, but that's a very minor hassle compared to scrubbing pots and constantly having to stand over your food to make sure it doesn't burn. I've already mentioned that I'm a lazy cook, and the BakePacker lets me kick back and enjoy myself or put up my tent while my food is cooking. For my money, the BakePacker is a hands-down favorite. It's quick, convenient, lightweight, and inexpensive.

The BakePacker comes in two sizes. The standard BakePacker weighs eight ounces and fits any seven-and-a-half-inch diameter straight-sided pot with a lid. The Ultra-Light BakePacker weighs only four ounces and fits any six-inch diameter straight-sided pot with a lid.

The Baking Skillet

Skillet baking is one of the older forms of baking, and one that I use quite frequently. I love my cast-iron skillet for baking cornbread in the oven, but with a little practice, you can bake biscuits, upside-down cakes, tea cakes, cookies, and just about anything you want, at home, on the trail, or on the water.

Skillet baking doesn't require a cast-iron skillet: You can use any kind of skillet. A heat diffuser, generally found at any store that handles kitchen supplies, is a real help if you cannot easily control your heat source. I bought my diffuser at

Cast-iron skillet resting on heat diffuser.

a grocery store for $3.99. It helps to evenly distribute the heat and results in a more evenly baked product.

Biscuits baked in a skillet are better than any baked in the oven. When I'm baking biscuits in my skillet, I usually brown them on one side then flip them over. Then I put a lid on the skillet and reduce the heat to low. The key to skillet baking is to stay with it from start to finish if you don't want burnt bread. There is nothing fast or labor-saving about it, but it has the advantage of using equipment you already have, with the possible exception of the heat diffuser.

The Rome Pie Iron

The Rome pie iron is designed for small baking tasks, such as sandwich toasting, over open flames. While the long handles limit the pie iron's convenience in terms of packing, they are an absolute necessity with open fires.

The Rome pie iron.

The two-piece unit opens up, and the hinge allows quick disassembly, so you can use both non-stick pans as separate long-handled frying pans. Small portions of a batter mixture—perhaps a half or two-thirds of a cup—could easily be placed in the pie iron and held in a fire.

Frequent turning and peeking would allow you to bake with relative convenience.

The Banks Fry-Bake

This baking system consists of a base pan (which can double as a frying pan) and a tight-fitting lid with a special-purpose, shallow, circular well around its perimeter. The entire unit is composed of anodized aluminum so you don't

The Banks Fry-Bake. The ridge on top allows it to hold hot coals.

have to worry about scratching the surface of the pan and creating areas where your baked goods will stick. This is a baking pan that truly lives up to its claim of great construction and ease of use. This product is built to last.

The shallow well in the lid makes it easy to place glowing coals, or even build a small fire of twigs, for even baking. As your camp stove heats the bottom of the pan, the twig fire heats the top. Incidentally, the old method of giving the pan a quarter-turn every now and again to ensure even baking on the bottom is still an excellent idea. Even though you have to watch this baking device to prevent burning or scorching, it is an excellent pan and one I do not hesitate to recommend highly.

The Boma

The Boma stainless steel cooker from South Africa has a truncated, funnel-shaped firebox. It is well insulated with vermiculite and has a convenient door. With its wide variety of smoking, baking, and cooking options, the Boma would make an excellent choice for cabin, beach, boating,

The Boma, complete with cooking accessories.

or base camp. It can also double as a safe space-heater—on deck while berthed in calm weather—to extend your boating season a bit, or in a properly ventilated enclosure (that is, one with a hood or chimney attached directly above the cooker).

The system comprises the stove, an ash tray, a pot ring and grill, a large, triangular stove top, a five-liter pot with a lid, and two three-liter pots with lids. Stainless steel construction throughout means that one can safely use wood, charcoal, or even coal as fuel. Three steel angle irons inside the top of the firebox allow the five-liter pot to rest safely about three inches below the opening, protecting the sides of the pot from cooling winds and thus conserving fuel—if you've used a Trangia, system 25 or 27, you'll be familiar with the idea. The smaller pots could be used in the same manner, but they wouldn't be as stable, and I'd recommend against the practice.

Inverting any of the pots over the grill allows you to smoke foods, while careful control of the fire should also permit baking directly on the grill, or baking by using two pots in a double-boiler arrangement.

For those who wish to combine modern efficiency with more traditional stewpot cooking, a size #1 Platpotjie (see page 19) fits neatly into the Boma stove for efficient simmering or cast-iron baking as well.

The BushBaker

The BushBaker is a fourteen-ounce, steam-baking system that basically creates a double-boiler, with the interior pot resembling a tube cake pan. The unit assembles neatly and quickly, and the parts nest inside the pot of the baker/steamer. The unit requires the use of a heat diffuser because high tempera-

The BushBaker system with bundling strap.

tures can melt the saucepan. The manufacturers recommend that you make a heat diffuser by taking an empty sixteen-ounce steel can and removing both ends completely. Lay the can on its side, smash it flat, and you have a perfectly dandy heat diffuser.

When I used the BushBaker, I made a good heat diffuser from a clean bean can, removing the label first. It was fairly easy to use, but as I've mentioned before, I'm a peeker when I cook. This unit seemed to cook the top of my first cake quickly to about one-third of its depth. It was baked deeply enough for the cake to spring back to the touch, which is a standard oven test for sufficient cooking. Unfortunately, it wasn't done on the bottom, as determined by the straw test method, in which you pierce the cake with a straw, toothpick, or thin twig. When you withdraw it, small particles of the cake will stick to the straw if it isn't fully done. It took about forty minutes to cook the cake after subtracting the five minutes lost when I peeked and thought it was done.

This cooker would be OK for a galley, cabin, or base camp. Because of the longer cooking times, it uses a considerable amount of fuel. I was also concerned by the idea that the saucepan would melt on high heat without a heat diffuser. A lot of the hikers I've talked to have trouble controlling the flame on their stoves. Fuel use and safety should be carefully considered. This unit could not be used on open fires because of the temperature restrictions. The manufacturer says it plans to switch to a stainless steel pot in the near future. I feel that such a move will create a much safer unit.

The Common Double Boiler

If you have a nesting cookset, you can use the pots for baking. This is a very common method of baking, and has a long history. You can use water in the bottom pot, or you can use a heat diffuser. I also use parchment paper in the top pot to make for easy removal of the baked item and convenient cleaning. Like the Bush-Baker, it takes a little longer to bake, but it will work just fine. It requires no extra purchase, unless you want to use parchment paper as I do, but it will need more fuel, so I don't recommend it for frequent use during long trips.

I also recommend that you don't fill the baking (inner) pot more than one-third full with batter. In this instance, less is better because you can cook two thin items in less time than you can cook one thick item. Also, the thicker the mix, the less likely it is that the bread will get done in the center. I feel certain that this factor is what prompted the makers of the BushBaker to use a tube pan for their insert, so the heat could circulate up the tube to prevent uneven cooking and undone centers.

A ten-inch, traditional, footed
cast-iron Dutch oven, from GSI.

A footed, twelve-inch Dutch oven
in cast aluminum, from GSI.

A ten-inch, cast aluminum
Dutch oven without feet,
from GSI.

A nontraditional, multipurpose,
cast aluminum Dutch oven with
optional, nonstick griddle top,
from Rome.

Dutch Ovens

A prized possession of early explorers, pioneers, and mountain
men and women, the Dutch oven is a valuable tool for both home
cooking and the great outdoors. It offers limitless versatility in
cooking styles and can be used directly on an open fire, camp
stove, or stove top.

Traditional Dutch ovens were made from cast iron. Even
though it's heavy, it offers excellent heat conduction and even
heating. For trips where weight is not a problem (with pack animals or on watercraft) the Dutch oven is a very desirable piece of
equipment. It's not a backpacking oven, though, unless you are
Arnold Schwarzenegger. It's great for boats, base camps, hunting
lodges, and RVs.

The aluminum Dutch oven is the newest addition to the Dutch
oven evolution. It tips the scales at about one-third the weight of
a cast-iron oven of similar size. Its light weight and quick-heating

properties make it quite efficient. The reduction in weight means that not only can boaters, campers, lodges and RVs use it, but it's also a reasonable burden on short backpacking trips.

Both iron and aluminum Dutch ovens come in two diameters, ten inches and twelve inches. There are also optional pieces of baking equipment you can buy to use with these ovens, including a lid lifter and a wire rack.

The Platpotjie

The Platpotjie (pronounced PLAT-poi-kee) is a flat-bottomed variation of the traditional South African potjie or cooking pot. As indicated earlier, both the legged and the legless versions of Dutch ovens have their followers. Each offers a unique form that lends itself to slightly different cooking styles. We should note here that the Platpotjie fits neatly into the Boma stainless steel cooker, nestling in the open top. There are brackets inside the top opening that hold the pot. This makes an already efficient cooker even more so.

The Platpotjie, a flat-bottomed South African traditional cooking pot.

Once properly seasoned, this device should provide many generations of use, on or off the trail or boat. A wide range of Platpotjie sizes is available.

The Potjie

This pot predates the eighteenth-century "spider" style Dutch ovens used in early American homes either directly over the fire in the hearth or chafing-dish style with a fire directly under it. The major difference,

The Potjie, the legendary, three-legged, South African cast-iron pot, is ideal for small fires and big meals. Its legs are longer than most, enabling you to build and feed a small fire directly under the pot and encircle it with stones.

aside from the shape, is the long skillet-style handle on the spider.

For the outdoor baker, the Potjie offers efficiency and convenience. Potjies are available in a very wide range of sizes from about three pounds to almost one hundred and forty pounds.

The Folding Reflector Oven

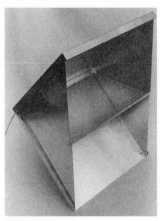

Mechanically, this oven from E-Z Camping works similarly to the Sun Oven described later in this chapter. The big difference is that it reflects the heat of an open fire, rather than the heat of the sun. You must be careful to position the reflector oven correctly for maximum efficiency; and be aware that the food closest to the fire may cook faster than the rest, requiring you to rotate the pan for even cooking. But before you adjust a reflector oven, remember that you're handling very hot metal. A regular oven thermometer placed on the shelf of the oven works well.

E-Z Camping's aluminum folding reflector oven.

This unit, one of several similar ovens available from different manufacturers or easily fabricated at home, is easy to assemble and folds to about three-quarters of an inch thick by thirteen-and-a-half inches square for convenient storage. Unfolded, the two-pound, three-ounce reflector oven measures eighteen-and-three-quarter by thirteen-and-a-half by thirteen-and-a-half inches.

Using the reflector oven takes practice, but once you've gained a little experience baking with it, you can cook almost anything you want with a little effort. In favor of the reflector oven is the fact that you are using a heat source (an open fire) which may be available anyway for heat or comfort. Of course, this isn't the most convenient baking device for a quick luncheon bread, but it could be a handy piece of equipment for cabins (use it in front of the fireplace), car camping, winter backpacking, or in base camps.

The OutBack Oven

Basically a skillet baker with bells and whistles, Cascade Design's Traveling Light OutBack Oven is a Teflon-coated pan and lid with an off/bake/burn thermometer attached as a lid handle. It has an aluminum heat diffuser, and a nicely insulated, dome-shaped shield that covers the entire baking pan. They call this cover a pot parka, and I think it is one of the better parts of this ensemble. As with many of the other cookers, it takes practice with the OutBack to be

The OutBack Oven system. The pan and cover (left), the heat diffuser, and reflector. The insulating "pot parka" is at the rear.

able to cook your breads without burning or scorching them. The trick with this equipment is to stay with it from start to finish.

As with the skillet, the OutBack Oven is capable of cooking a wide variety of items successfully if you tend it carefully. The pot parka helps conserve fuel by retaining the heat—but the oven has caused some overheating problems for stoves with integral fuel tanks. The manufacturer now includes a template and some aluminum sheet for a reflector collar. You must cut the collar to fit snugly, so there's no danger of the heat reflecting back from the diffuser to the fuel tank. This same problem would hold true if you used the pot parka to improve and conserve the fuel usage on any other baker. This could be a serious hazard, so do make sure you prepare the reflector as directed. The company also recommends that the oven system not be used with the older Svea stoves. I'd recommend that you use only stoves with separate fuel bottles. If you are a gadget person, you will like the OutBack Oven and all its parts.

If you're not a gadget person, I recommend the Ultralight OutBack Oven that lets you use your own pan. This unit is well constructed and has other optional accessories. A convenient mesh bag is included in the system.

The OutBack Oven comes in three models:
- The Outfitter, the largest of the group, cooks for four and weighs three pounds.
- The Plus Ten cooks for two and weighs one-and-a-half pounds.
- The Ultralight requires that you use your own pot, but includes the diffuser, parka, and reflector.

Pressure Cookers

Pressure cooking and baking uses high temperature and pressure to cook quickly. Steam is locked in the pot by a gasketed lid. There is also a release valve to prevent pressure build-up and explosions. Some valves have gauges so you can select the pressure. Some of the newer pressure cookers have self-regulating valves for optimal cooking.

My three favorite pressure cookers.

I have three pressure cookers; one holds four quarts, one holds six quarts, and the other a quart-and-a-half. The latter looks like a large skillet, and cooks even faster than the four-quart cooker by dispersing the food over a comparatively large shallow area. I use it almost every day at home. The pressure cooker is ideal for base camps, hunting lodges, boat galleys, RVs, and car camping. It is very versatile and built to last. I've had my four-quart Mirro since 1967, and have only had to replace the pressure valve once. I've had my smaller cooker, a Kuhn-Rikon, for five years and I've replaced the lid seal gasket once. I've had my six-quart Mirro about a year. Most pressure cookers are made of aluminum or stainless steel. International Presto Industries offers both, Mirro Cookware offers aluminum, while Kuhn-Rikon, a Swiss company, offers only stainless steel. The aluminum cooker is naturally lighter in weight.

Cooking with a pressure cooker is not like cooking with any other type of cooker. For a start, your timing needs to be more exact so you don't overcook your food. Once the pressure has built up, you can't open the cooker until the contents have cooled down and all the pressure has been released. As you raise the pressure, you also raise the temperature at which water will boil—normally 212 degrees F (at ordinary atmospheric pressure at sea level). Boiling temperature decreases at high altitudes. In a pressure cooker at fifteen pounds per square inch water can be heated to 250 degrees F. The raised pressure and temperature inside the cooker break down the food fiber very quickly while locking in the nutrients and flavors that are normally lost. If you're not yet using a pressure cooker at home, I highly recommend you get one. It will save you hours in the kitchen. Incidentally, if the reason you aren't using one is because you're afraid it will explode, let me reassure you: I've not had a single explosion in the twenty-eight years I've been using them.

Baking in a pressure cooker is easy, but don't expect to produce yeast rolls. Instead, choose items that are meant to be steamed, like Boston Brown Bread or date-nut bread.

My four-quart Mirro aluminum pressure cooker weighs in at slightly more than three and one-half pounds; the six-quart Mirro at a little more than four and three-quarters pounds. My one-and-a-half-quart Kuhn stainless cooker weighs nearly six pounds. Though pressure cookers aren't inexpensive, they're built to last. I can't say enough good things about them—but try one for yourself. Experiencing is believing.

The Pyromid Folding Oven

The Pyromid is a folding, portable, stainless steel barbecue stove. Unlike the other baking devices I've mentioned, this is a complete stove system, with optional attachments for the three larger models that enable you to do large batches of baking, roasting, smoking, and so on.

Pyromid's folding system. The oven is at left, the stove is at the rear, and the stove lid is at right. The entire system fits into the small black bag at right rear. The small items in the center are aluminum foil liners and fire starters.

The Pyromid system is designed to use charcoal briquettes fitting vertically into two fuel grates. This will give you either even heat over a long period for baking or high temperatures over a shorter period for grilling. You could also fuel it with wood chunks or twigs, although you'd probably lose some control over temperatures.

This stove is very versatile, and it's easy to set up and dismantle. For baking purposes, the included baking hood works quite well, and the optional smoker hood unit has multiple shelves, making it easy to bake both an entree and a bread or a dessert at the same time, using temperatures up to 400 degrees F. A detailed instruction manual describes how to place the charcoal for various temperatures.

The entire unit is of stainless steel construction (which makes it heavy) and has disposable aluminum foil liners under the fuel grate for easy clean-up of ashes and food residue. Although the liner is handy, you might consider packing the ash and food residue in one barrier bag and the aluminum liners in a separate barrier bag for recycling when you return home. I love the versatility of the Pyromid, and think you could enjoy its convenience at home as well as on the go.

The Pyromid system is available in four sizes measuring eight, twelve, fifteen, and eighteen inches but the eight-inch model is available only in a stove configuration.

Coleman's Folding Campstove

The aluminum Campstove oven by Coleman folds cleverly, with space for the single shelf to be stored inside the folded oven. Four alignment tongues at top and bottom fit into slots on the folding sides and hold the opened oven square, while two lever-style latches fasten the unit securely. These same latches also lock the oven in the folded position when you stow it away for travel. It is very nicely made and well thought out.

While there is only a single shelf in the Coleman, it will adequately hold eight-inch baking trays or loaf pans, and the top of the oven can serve as a warming griddle for side dishes, or as a place to set bread

Coleman's folding Camp-stove oven. Note the heat diffuser on the bottom, and the single shelf.

dough to rise. A heat deflector in the bottom of the oven acts as a diffuser and should protect baked goods from burning at all except the most intense heats. A thermometer is built into the door and a lever-type latch holds it tightly closed.

The design of the Coleman oven, while recommended for Coleman stoves, should be perfect for a wide range of similar stoves if you use them with care. But I wouldn't recommend you use it with more intense heat sources or open flames.

Sportsman and Outfitter Ovens

These ovens from Fox Hill Corporation are constructed of heavy-gauge aluminum and come complete with wire shelves and baking pans. The Sportsman model has one shelf inside and the Outfitter model has two shelves. The shelves are attached directly to the lid, making it very convenient to remove hot pans.

The ovens have a temperature gauge conveniently mounted on the front, chromed baking rack(s) attached to the lid, and non-stick baking pan(s). You carefully lift the lid to expose the baking racks. There is an empty space

The Outfitter oven (right) has two shelves for increased baking room. The Sportsman (left) lies on its side to display the diffuser on the bottom.

between the base of the oven and the racks where a deflector shields the pans from direct stove heat to protect your food from scorching. The temperature gauge allows you to bake at the same temperature you would in your home oven. If your recipe calls for 350 degrees F for twenty minutes, that's exactly how long you cook it in the Sportsman or Outfitter ovens: There's no need for special recipe conversions. The oven requires only one burner on a camp stove. It also works well on propane stoves, wood stoves, gas or electric stoves, and a variety of other stoves.

In 1993 we had a blizzard here in western North Carolina. We were without power for almost eight days and we used a Fox Hill Outfitter oven the whole time. Actually, I was in bed with double pneumonia, and Sam, Ward, and Laura (my husband and children) did all the cooking. We have a gas stovetop that can be lit with a match if the power is off. What a lifesaver it is. Because the Fox Hill oven cooks like a regular oven, we just set it on top of our gas stovetop, and we had an oven with two shelves for cooking. We also have friends who use it on top of their wood-burning stove.

Because this oven is not collapsible, it's not for the long-distance hiker, unless you set up a base camp. The Fox Hill oven is for the weekend camper, car camper, RV traveler, boat galley, or, in our case, emergency backup for the snowbound where power outages are frequent. It is also great for hunting trips. We love our Sportsman oven, and I wouldn't want to go through a winter in the mountains without it. I think those of you who have boats, campers, and RVs really should check this oven out.

Both ovens are ten inches square. The Sportsman is six inches high and weighs two pounds, eleven ounces. The Outfitter is approximately ten inches high and weighs four pounds, two ounces. Both ovens include eight-inch square, non-stick baking pans. A carrying case is optional.

The Sun Oven

The Sun Oven, from Burns-Milwaukee, Inc., uses solar power and looks like an old-style chest cooler. It measures approximately nineteen-and-a-half inches square by fifteen inches deep. The interior space for cooking is approximately twelve-and-a-half inches by nine inches, with adequate height clearance of about eight inches. The folding aluminum panels open up to become the reflecting unit. It comes with an oven temperature gauge, a self-leveling shelf inside, and a glass oven door that is perfect for us peekers. It weighs in at eighteen pounds-eight ounces and is too cumbersome for hikers and backpackers, but not for boating, remote cabins, base camps, weekend car-camping, gunkholing, beach cooking, or pack-animal trips. Since it is dependent on sunshine, however, you'd need a back-up system for rainy, overcast days. This is also the perfect emergency or survival oven for solar purists.

Side view of the closed Sun Oven. Note adjustable grooves for changing the angle to gain maximum efficiency.

The Sun Oven open for business.

What can I say, except that I fell in love with this oven? I baked bread in it, cooked pizza, and warmed leftovers. Since it used no fuel except sunshine, I did not feel guilty when it took forty-five minutes to cook homemade yeast bread. I have to admit it's more expensive than the average boating/backpacking oven, but with sufficient usage it could pay for itself—after all, you never have to buy fuel for it.

Sam, who designed our solar home, was impressed with this oven's performance. He discovered that in August it would heat up to 350 degrees F in ten minutes. On a sunny but windy day in January, with an outdoor temperature of only 38 degrees F, the unit heated from 70 degrees F to 140 degrees F in ten minutes. After another ten minutes, it reached 165 degrees F. In a total of thirty minutes in the late afternoon sun, it went from 70 degrees F to 180 degrees F. At that stage, the oven's angle to the sun was adjusted, and the temperature rose to 210 degrees at forty minutes, 220 degrees at fifty minutes, and 240 degrees at sixty minutes. While these temperatures are too modest for most baking, a slowly cooked stew would be a tasty meal on such a cold blustery winter afternoon. It is also likely that beginning the cooking at about noon would have increased temperatures significantly, perhaps even to baking levels.

When you do use this oven, you have to set its solar collector to the best angle, and it should be adjusted every fifteen or twenty minutes to keep it facing the sun.

NON-TRADITIONAL AND HOMEMADE BAKING DEVICES

Rock Baking

Food has probably been cooked on hot rocks as long as it has been cooked in thermal springs or over planned fires. But a few notes of caution are in order. Don't use rocks taken directly out of a stream—they might

Simple bread on a hot rock.

explode as the moisture trapped in them builds up steam pressure or uneven heat-expansion pressure. Keep in mind that the smaller the mineral crystals are in the rock, the smaller the pores available to hold water. These types of rocks are less likely to explode. But it's more complicated than that, and you should be cautious. If you are really interested in this type of cooking, try checking with the college or university geology department nearest you for advice and geological survey maps.

The shape of the rock you need depends on the type of bread you want to bake. It's also important for the rock to be relatively thin—about two or three inches thick is about right—if you want to use it directly over the fire as a skillet.

For some types of bread, it's best to build the fire directly against a large, rounded rock. Dough, like that for flour tortillas, is flattened very thin and then literally slapped onto the hot rock. As it cooks, it separates itself from the rock. Obviously, this type of cooking is best for thin, flat breads and crackers.

Stick Baking

If you've ever roasted marshmallows over a fire, you know how to use a stick for baking. Most Boy Scouts and Girl Scouts have probably cooked stick bread (bread dough wrapped around a stick) over an open campfire. It's quick and easy. The only things you need are a good fire, a green-wood stick (long enough so you don't burn yourself), and dough that's pliable enough to cling to the stick and light enough to cook quickly. Canned biscuits rolled in cinnamon and sugar, or homemade pizza dough mixed with sausage and cheese are some of my favorites for stick baking.

Hearty bread dough on a stick. The stove is a folding pocket cooker from Amgazit.

Gallon-Size Tin Can Ovens

Most restaurants use items that come in gallon-size (#10) cans and will gladly supply you with all the cans you want, just for the asking. But beware—don't use cans that have ever contained something other than food. Cans previously used for paint, varnish, fuel, and so on could create a variety of problems, including poisoning, poisonous gases, and even explosions.

Two versions of "ovens" made from #10 cans are shown and described below, but I'd guess many other similar (and more elaborate) ovens could be made using the same materials. Both versions use only two #10 cans, a bit of aluminum foil, plus a smaller can or a loaf pan for the bread. Both ovens may be used with any of the heat sources already mentioned, but pay careful attention to the baking time, which depends on how much heat is being generated.

A vertical #10 can oven. It's likely that only one end will have been removed from any can you get. To make the first of these two ovens, you then should cut the lower can with snips and bend a flap up from the side to permit ventilation, as shown. This will become the lower can in which the coals are placed. Make a hole or holes in the side above the ventilation flap with a piercing can opener. Don't make any holes in the can end, however. The side vents will let smoke escape and provide cross-ventilation.

A vertical oven made from #10 cans.

Remove both ends from the second can, and pierce it several times about its circumference using a can opener or knife. Use the rings on the can to keep the piercings level. After each piercing of the can, twist the opener to create small ledges inside the can (note the dent created on the outside of the upper can in the photo). The lid of the can that you cut out is placed on these ledges. The second can, the "oven," is then placed on the top of the first. You can place your dough directly on this can lid resting on the ledges, or you can put the dough in a smaller can and lower it onto the shelf in the upper can. Cover the top with a piece of foil to retain the heat.

If you cannot conveniently create the ledges or remove the end of the second can, simply place the second can, open end up, on top of the first. Now put a few pebbles in the bottom of the upper can to keep the small baking container from getting too hot on the bottom, and to allow for more even baking. If you grease the small baking can, or line it with baking paper or foil, you'll find it easier to remove the finished food.

A horizontal #10 can oven. You can make the second simple #10 oven by removing both ends from one can and carefully bending the top (it takes some effort) to make a "V" or "U" shape to cradle the upper can in a horizontal position—see the photo. This creates a sturdy base, provides for exhaust, and concentrates the heat at the top. You can cut a flap in the lower can if necessary (as in the lower can of the vertical oven) to feed the heat source.

The second can is simply placed horizontally in this cradle and used as the oven. One of the removed ends may be bent slightly twice, creating two opposing edges, to make a shelf (see photo) for holding your bread dough or a bread pan. Use a piece of foil over the open end to contain the heat. Again, it will be necessary to watch the bread and the heat source carefully to make sure your food is fully cooked but not burned.

A #10 can horizontal oven.

Small pit fires or short trench fires will work well for these ovens, but only when conditions (and laws) safely permit open fires. (Use rocks to contain the fire and stabilize the cans.) It's interesting to know that even a candle will provide enough heat to bake a biscuit in the upper can, and to fry bacon and eggs on the top of the lower can. It's a slow but successful process that might amaze a friend and stimulate some serious conversation, whether you're deep in the woods or on a beach near your favorite gunkhole. Cooking with cans is appropriate in some situations, especially when you have no time constraints, but it's also good to know about it so you can use it in emergencies.

The Hay-Box Overnight Cooker

I read about the hay-box overnight cooker in a hard-bound book of the 1855 *Ladies Godey Magazine*. The cooker takes several days to make, and it's constructed as follows:

Select a box (preferably wooden) and a covered pot you wish to cook in. Place the empty pot in the box, and pack hay (or shredded newspaper) around it and over it. Wet the hay down and compress it. Then set the whole box in the sun to dry, and do not remove the pot. The next day, after the hay has dried, pack more hay in the box, wet it down again, and compress the hay again. Set the box in the sun to dry as before. Continue to do this until the box is filled completely to the top with very densely compressed dry hay. Now you must cut out a section of the hay directly above the pot and remove the pot. Your super-insulated hay-box cooker is complete.

To use the hay-box cooker, simply place your food in the pot

CAN YOU CARRY IT?

Weights and Dimensions of Baking Devices

Round or Oval Baking Equipment	Diameter (Inches)	Height (Inches)	Weight (Pounds)
10-inch aluminum oven	10	5⅞	3.32
BushBaker[1]	8¼	4⅛	1
10-inch iron Dutch oven	10¼	8	14.35
12-inch aluminum Dutch oven	12	7½	6.3
Platpotjie[1], #1 size	19	5⅝	11.43
Potjie[1], #2 size	9¾	10	18.83
BakePacker, Standard	7⅜	1⅞	0.5
BakePacker, Ultralight	5¾	2³⁄₁₆	0.25
Boma stainless cooker[2]	12½	16½	15.32
OutBack Oven[1]	10	1⅝	1.63

Square or Rectangular Baking Equipment	Width (Inches)	Depth (Inches)	Height (Inches)	Weight (Pounds)
Reflector oven	18¾	9½	13½	2.19
Coleman Folding Campstove	12⅛	12¼	12¼	6.76
Rome Pie Iron[1]	8⅝	6¼	1½	1.79
Sportsman oven	10⅜	10⅜	6⅛	3.18
Outfitter oven	10⅜	10⅜	9½	4.92
Pyramid oven	11½	11½	10¼	6.65
Pyramid stove	11½	11½	11	6.04
Sun Oven	22	19½	14	18.5

Notes:
[1] Handles are not included in the dimensions.
[2] Weight does not include three pots and triangle stove top.
Measurements are all outside dimensions, and are made at the longest line of any dimension to include knobs, thermometers, and similar protrusions.

(not yet in the hay-box) and bring the contents up to as high a temperature as you can with a roaring boil. Next, you place the covered pot of food in the hay-box, and cover it with the section of hay you cut out. By next day, the food will be ready. But before serving it, you should bring it back to a boil for at least ten minutes to kill any bacteria that might have grown during the slow cooking process.

I think the hay-box would have been especially helpful to a bread baker who depended on a sourdough starter that had to stay warm and develop into a sponge before the mixing of the bread could take place. It would also be an excellent place to put the bread dough to rise.

No, I haven't lost my senses. I realize you couldn't conveniently take the hay-box on backpacking trips and such, but I couldn't resist the urge to share it with you. Maybe it will come in handy for a cabin, hunting, keeping a beverage warm if you forgot a thermos, or cooking grains like oatmeal, or rice.

* CHAPTER 3 *
Yeast Breads

east is a living organism, a fungus, that makes bread dough rise. The growth of yeast produces a gas, carbon dioxide, that is captured in bubbles in the stretchy dough. As the bubbles grow, they expand the dough.

Each of the many different species of yeast acts differently and grows at a different rate. Most yeasts grow rapidly when they are moist, warm, and well fed. The warm water and flour in dough provide all these necessities.

For ease of measurement, I have listed the equivalent of one package of yeast as approximately one tablespoon, even though the true measurement is two and one-quarter teaspoons. It is simply easier to make one measurement, in or out of the field. The small amount of extra yeast won't affect the outcome of the recipe. I've used this equivalent for more than ten years now, and I feel it works just dandy.

BAKER'S YEAST

Commercial yeast, or baker's yeast, is selected for certain of its predictable growth characteristics and its individual taste. It allows the baker to know how long to let a bread "proof" (grow the yeast), how long to let the bread rise, and what flavor it will impart. It can be purchased in a number of forms, including quarter-ounce or one-pound packs and compressed cakes. But it is not only yeast that determines whether or not a bread will rise. Flour—or more accurately the amount of protein in flour that will dissolve to form the elastic material gluten—is equally important. If a flour does not have much gluten it will not rise much, if at all.

Hard/strong wheat flour has the most gluten (twelve to fifteen percent); soft/spring wheat has only eight to ten percent. The flour bag usually will indicate whether it is spring or winter wheat; specially marked bread flours with malt will give you the best results. King Arthur brand flour is particularly good. (The King Arthur Flour Company—1-800-827-6836—offers "The Baker's Catalogue," which contains every ingredient you'll ever need for baking breads.)

Some flours, such as rye, oat, potato, tapioca, corn, and rice have no gluten and must be combined with wheat or added gluten to produce a yeast-bread. Barley and buckwheat flours have small quantities of gluten, but not enough to produce a yeast-bread without adding gluten.

Regular baker's yeast will die if it's heated past 130 degrees F (54 degrees C). In cold temperatures, such as those normally found in refrigerators, it will become dormant.

Note: In the recipes that follow, regular active dry yeast is referred to as regular dry yeast, and rapid-rise dry yeast (often called instant yeast) is referred to as rapid-rise yeast.

One Rising, or Two?

Almost all the standard yeast-bread recipes advise letting the bread rise until it doubles in bulk, after which it should be punched down, or kneaded, to reduce its size, then left to rise again.

The purpose of the second kneading is to eliminate large air pockets in the dough. This process also redistributes the stretched gluten throughout the mixture, making a more consistent dough that will rise evenly and have a finer crumb.

This second rising period is fine, and even desirable if you have time. But most people on the trail or on a boat have plenty of other things to do. So I recommend that you leave off the second rising period for the yeast breads.

If your recipe demands a second rising, I can honestly say your bread will be just fine without it and you'll save a couple of hours of preparation time. I must admit that the bread may rise unevenly. And it may have a few holes in it. Is that a big deal? After all, you're not eating at a four-star restaurant. And you'll still have fresh, delicious bread.

Most of the time, even at home, I've given up the second rising period for my breads. They have not suffered, and neither have my family or my dinner guests.

I also find that a single rising takes a lot of stress out of baking bread. All you have to do is mix your dough, knead it well, and put it in a greased pan to rise. It allows you to mix up a loaf of bread within an hour of dinner if you use rapid-rise yeast, or within two hours if you use regular dry yeast.

If you use rapid-rise yeast and mix the dough as soon as you reach your camp site, the bread will be ready to bake by the time you have your camp set up. If you premixed your dry ingredients at home, add water to the mix in a plastic bag large enough to accommodate rising, then take a walk.

I use rapid-rise yeast almost all of the time now. On a warm day my bread will rise in forty-five minutes to one hour. I can make it faster this way than I can in my bread machine.

Usually, if I'm trying a new recipe, I follow the instructions the first time. The next time I bake that recipe I use rapid-rise yeast and forgo the second rising. I have never been disappointed. I'm sure that bread connoisseurs will consider me a heathen for suggesting that omitting the second rising makes no difference—but remember, we're talking here about baking in less than ideal conditions.

My other main suggestion is that you keep an extra package of yeast with you in case the package you use does not rise. Also carry some baking powder with you. The baking powder can be dissolved in a small amount of water and added to a yeast bread that didn't rise properly. It is especially useful if you have bread rising (supposedly) while you are out gathering wood for the fire and arrive back tired and hungry to discover your yeast didn't work. Most people would rather discard the mixture than wait another hour or so to eat. But you don't have to wait if you add baking powder. Naturally, your baking-powder bread won't be as wonderful as the yeast bread would have been; but ravenous hikers will still find it good to eat.

To remedy a dough that didn't rise, use approximately one teaspoon of baking powder per cup of flour used. Make a depression in the middle of the dough, add the baking powder and an equal amount of water, and mix thoroughly with your hands.

You can trust me on this one folks. Try it next time it happens to you. If you've never had a loaf of bread that didn't rise, you haven't baked bread very often. I bet it has even happened to Julia Child.

SOURDOUGH YEAST (WILD YEAST)

Wild yeast is everywhere. It's in the air all around us, on the leaves of plants, and on fruit. Unwashed grapes are a particularly rich source of wild yeast, but be careful to use grapes grown organically, without pesticides.

Wild yeast is as unpredictable as the weather. When you think you have all of a particular wild yeast's characteristics nailed down, it fools you. One loaf of bread may rise over the top of the pan; the next loaf, prepared the same way, may not even make it to the top of the pan.

Wild yeast is used in sourdough, and it's different in a major way from commercial yeast. It doesn't like as much warmth. It prefers a room temperature or a mild environment. It is very easy to kill sourdough yeast by adding water warmer than 70 degrees F. As with any other yeast, however, it will become dormant if the temperature is too cool.

One important thing I've learned about sourdough is that if you're not baking bread every day, the starter (see page 52) will grow quite large from just its regular feedings. Most recipes advise you to pour the extra starter away and keep only two cups, but I just can't bring myself to do that. Instead, I try to share it with all my friends and neighbors.

Nancy Silverton, in her book *Breads from La Brea Bakery*, seems to feel that the yeast reacts in an emotional way and is affected by its environment. Sound silly? Well, if you consider that yeast is a living organism, it doesn't sound silly at all. It seems that it should be expected. If you want to make sourdough bread, I highly recommend her book for additional reading.

PACKAGED-YEAST BREAD RECIPES

Beer Yeast Bread

Servings: Makes 10 to 12 small rolls

This bread has the convenience of a regular non-yeast quick bread but the flavor of a yeast roll. If you use water instead of beer, regular dry yeast gives it the same yeasty flavor—but remember, the yeast is there for its taste only. You don't have to wait for the mixture to rise like a yeast bread. This bread was quite popular in the seventies, and I have made it many times. With the availability of fast-acting yeast, we have a lot more options now, and I find I don't make this recipe very often, but it is still a great quick roll.

Ingredients	All-Dry
¼ cup olive oil	⅛ cup shortening powder
¼ teaspoon salt	¼ teaspoon
3 cups self-rising, enriched white flour	3 cups
¼ cup white granulated sugar	¼ cup
12 fluid ounces beer	
nil water	12 fluid ounces
nil dry yeast, rapid-rise or regular	1 teaspoon

Instructions: Mix all dry ingredients and olive oil together and then add the beer (or water). But omit the yeast if you use beer rather than water. The yeast is used only for flavor. Once you've mixed the dough to the consistency you want, drop a quarter-cup of dough into a small bowl of flour. Dust off any flour that does not stick, and shape into a ball. Place on a greased pan. Continue with remaining dough until all is shaped. It makes about a dozen rolls. Bake at 350 degrees F for twenty to thirty minutes.

Note: If you're using a deep baking dish, such as a Dutch oven, you can bake the dough as one large loaf.

Recipe Totals: 2,138 calories, 341 g carbohydrates (13 g dietary fiber and 68 g sugars), 0 g cholesterol, 58 g total fat (8 g saturated fat), 38 g protein, 5,313 mg sodium.

Dietary Exchanges (recipe totals): Bread, 17.5; Fat, 11.9; Fruit, 3.25; Lean Meat, 0; Milk, 0; Vegetables, 0.

Remember to divide totals by the number of servings.

Carol's Yeast Rolls

Servings: Makes 12 large or 16 small rolls

C arol and I graduated from college together with degrees in geology. We moved to Gwinnett County, Georgia, and lived about seven miles apart for five or six years. Needless to say, we got together often then. Now, fifteen or so years later, we are still good friends, though she is in Montana and I am in North Carolina.

Carol is an excellent cook. She gave me this roll recipe in 1973 and I have made it often for my family. It is like my mother's Angel Biscuit recipe in that the unused portion of the mixture can be refrigerated for as long as a week for daily use. It is very easy to make, and with rapid-rise yeast, you can have a dozen rolls in about forty-five minutes, including mixing, rising, and cooking time. Enjoy.

Ingredients	All-Dry
1 cup warm water	1¼ cups
⅛ cup vegetable shortening	⅛ cup shortening powder
3½ cups enriched flour	3½ cups
¼ cup white granulated sugar	¼ cup
1 teaspoon salt	1 teaspoon
¼-ounce package rapid-rise yeast	¼-ounce package (or 1 tablespoon)
1 raw whole egg, extra-large	2 tablespoons powder

(continued)

Instructions: Mix yeast, sugar, salt, and warm water. Add the egg and one-eighth cup shortening. Gradually mix in flour. Mix well. Cover with a piece of plastic wrap and a damp towel. Place in the refrigerator until ready to use. When ready to use, pinch dough off for each roll. Place on a greased pan or in greased muffin tins. Let rise about thirty minutes, but if you're using regular yeast instead of rapid-rise, let rise until double in size—about two hours. Bake at 400 degrees F for fifteen minutes.

Recipe Totals: 2,118 calories, 393 g carbohydrates (14 g dietary fiber and 58 g sugars), 247 mg cholesterol, 36 g total fat (8 g saturated fat), 57 g protein, 2,220 mg sodium.

Dietary Exchanges (recipe totals): Bread, 19.7; Fat, 5.58; Fruit, 3.25; Lean Meat, 1.1; Milk, 0; Vegetables, 0.

Remember to divide totals by the number of servings.

Cheesy Pepper Bread

Servings: Makes two small loaves of six to eight slices each

S picy bread is always popular with my family. We like this bread with any meal. It is especially good with Huevos Rancheros (Ranch Eggs) or chili.

Ingredients	All-Dry
¼-ounce package rapid-rise yeast	¼-ounce package (or 1 tablespoon)
¼ cup warm water	1¼ cups
2⅓ cups enriched flour	2⅓ cups
1 teaspoon salt	1 teaspoon
⅛ cup white granulated sugar	⅛ cup
¼ teaspoon baking soda	¼ teaspoon
1 cup cultured sour cream	½ cup powder
1 raw whole egg, extra-large	⅛ cup powder
1 cup Cheddar cheese, shredded	½ cup freeze-dried
1 teaspoon black pepper	1 teaspoon

Instructions: Grease two one-pound coffee cans. Combine yeast, sugar, and warm water. Set aside. Combine remaining dry ingredients and gradually mix in yeast mixture. Knead several times then divide in half and put in the coffee cans to rise for thirty to forty minutes until double in bulk. Bake at 350 degrees F for thirty-five to forty minutes. Cool before slicing.

Recipe Totals: 2,227 calories, 269 g carbohydrates (10 g dietary fiber and 42 g sugars), 27 g cholesterol, 95 g total fat (56 g saturated fat), 79 g protein, 3,360 mg sodium.

Dietary Exchanges (recipe totals): Bread, 13.1; Fat, 15.1; Fruit, 1.63; Lean Meat, 5.06; Milk, 0.92; Vegetables, 0.

Remember to divide totals by the number of servings.

Dijon Ham & Swiss Loaf

Servings: Makes four flower-pot loaves or one large loaf. Serves four.

With this recipe, you can bake your whole lunch at once. At home, I like to bake this in small terra-cotta flower pots. You can vary the filling to suit your individual taste or mood. As the dough is warmed over boiling water to help make the yeast rise more quickly, this is not a time-consuming bread to make.

Ingredients	All-Dry
(1) Bread Mix:	
3 cups all-purpose, enriched white flour	3 cups
⅛ cup white granulated sugar	2 tablespoons
½ teaspoon salt	½ teaspoon
2 × ¼-ounce packages dry active baker's yeast	2 × ¼-ounce packages
2 tablespoons margarine, unsalted	2 tablespoons powder
1 cup warm water	1 cup
(2) Filling:	
1½ cups cooked whole ham, trimmed but not heated	¾ cup freeze-dried
1 cup shredded Swiss cheese	½ cup freeze-dried
½ cup dill pickle slices	1 large single pickle
¼ cup Dijon mustard	⅛ cup mustard powder
nil water	1 cup

Instructions:

(1) Bread Mix: Combine warm water, sugar, and yeast and set aside. Combine flour, salt, and butter. Gradually add yeast mixture. Place in double boiler over boiling water for fifteen minutes to rise. Remove dough and knead until smooth. Roll out to fourteen inches by twelve inches.

(continued)

(2) **Filling:** Combine ham, Swiss cheese, and dill pickle slices. Spread bread dough with mustard and filling mixture. Roll into a loaf and bake at 375 degrees F for twenty-five minutes. For a glazed finish, brush the top of the loaf with egg yolk before baking.

Note: If you're using all-dry ingredients for the filling, let the ham and cheese rehydrate for about five minutes in cold water. Then drain all but one tablespoon of excess water and add the powdered mustard and the pickle plus one tablespoon of pickle juice.

Recipe Totals: 2,510 calories, 330 g carbohydrates (18 g dietary fiber and 37 g sugars), 208 mg cholesterol, 74 g total fat (29 g saturated fat), 126 g protein, 7,056 mg sodium.

Dietary Exchanges (recipe totals): Bread, 17; Fat, 8.33; Fruit, 1.63; Lean Meat, 11.7; Milk, 0; Vegetables, 2.18.

Remember to divide totals by the number of servings.

Crispy Hush Puppies

Servings: Makes 16 to 24 hush puppies

Most of the time I could make a meal of hush puppies alone, but fish is good too, especially if you have caught your own. This is a great mixture to dip chunks of fish in before deep-frying.

Ingredients	All-Dry
1 cup white, enriched, self-rising cornmeal	1 cup
1 cup enriched flour	1 cup
2 teaspoons double-acting baking powder	2 teaspoons
1 tablespoon white granulated sugar	1 tablespoon
½ teaspoon salt	½ teaspoon
1 raw whole egg, extra-large	2 tablespoons powder
⅓ cup raw onions, chopped	⅛ cup dried
1 teaspoon rapid-rise yeast	1 teaspoon
6 fluid ounces beer	1½ cups water
¼ cup olive oil	⅛ cup butter powder

extra olive oil, or packet of mayonnaise, for frying

Instructions: Combine all dry ingredients then add wet ingredients. Drop by the tablespoonful into oil heated for ten minutes. Turn over once to brown evenly. Drain on paper towels before serving.

Recipe Totals: 1,589 calories, 213 g carbohydrates (14 g dietary fiber and 27 g sugars), 247 mg cholesterol, 65 g total fat (8 g saturated fat), 38 g protein, 3,653 mg sodium.
Dietary Exchanges (recipe totals): Bread, 6.1; Fat, 11.8; Fruit, 0.813; Lean Meat, 1.1; Milk, 0; Vegetables, 1.06.
Remember to divide totals by the number of servings.

Dill Casserole Bread

Servings: Makes six to eight servings

This bread has a wonderful flavor. With nothing other than fruit and cheese it makes a great meal. I like it with vegetable soup, but it would be good with just about anything.

Ingredients	All-Dry
¼-ounce package rapid-rise yeast	1 tablespoon
2½ cups enriched flour	2½ cups
1 cup small-curd, creamed cottage cheese	½ cup freeze-dried
2 tablespoons white granulated sugar	⅛ cup
1 tablespoon chopped raw onions	1 teaspoon dehydrated
1 tablespoon butter oil (ghee)	1 tablespoon powder
2 teaspoons dill seed	2 teaspoons
1 teaspoon salt	1 teaspoon
1 teaspoon baking soda	1 teaspoon
1 raw whole egg, extra-large	⅛ cup powder
¼ cup warm water	1 cup

Instructions: Combine yeast, flour, sugar, salt, and warm water. Mix well, then add cottage cheese, baking soda, onion, dill seed, butter oil, and egg. Knead about five minutes or until well blended. Place dough in a well-oiled bread pan or Dutch oven. Let rise forty to forty-five minutes then bake at 400 degrees F for twenty to thirty minutes.

Recipe Totals: 1,694 calories, 281 g carbohydrates (11 g dietary fiber and 38 g sugars), 311 mg cholesterol, 32 g total fat (16 g saturated fat), 72 g protein, 4,333 mg sodium.
Dietary Exchanges (recipe totals): Bread, 14.1; Fat, 2.58; Fruit, 1.63; Lean Meat, 5.1; Milk, 0; Vegetables, 0.125.
Remember to divide totals by the number of servings.

Grandmother's Crumpets

Servings: Makes 12 crumpets

I've noticed over the past five to ten years an increasing interest in heirloom recipes—and not just on a personal level. Some of the priciest gourmet catalogs sell crumpets and similar fare made from old family recipes.

This is a true heirloom recipe. It was written on a scrap of paper that fell out of a cookbook once owned by my grandmother, Fanny Bell. My mother, Mary F. Bell, gave the cookbook to my oldest sister, Mary. Sister (that's what we've always called her) gave the book to me a number of years back. It's so old that it's literally falling apart. The spine and cover of the book are missing, along with the first thirty or forty pages. I don't even know its title or who the author was. Nonetheless, I treasure this old book and the recipes that were stuffed inside.

Ingredients	All-Dry
4 cups enriched flour	4 cups
1 cup whole milk	⅓ cup powder
¼-ounce package rapid-rise yeast	¼-ounce package (or 1 tablespoon)
2 raw whole eggs, extra-large	4 tablespoons powder
1 teaspoon salt	1 teaspoon
¾ cup water	2¼ cups

Instructions: Make a stiff batter and let it rise for thirty minutes or until it's light. Spoon batter into muffin rings on a hot griddle, or cook by the spoonful on a greased skillet. Bake slowly and brown on both sides.

Note: The original recipe called for one quart of flour and three-quarters of a cup of liquid yeast instead of the above ingredients.

Recipe Totals: 2,157 calories, 404 g carbohydrates (17 g dietary fiber and 21 g sugars), 527 mg cholesterol, 25 g total fat (9 g saturated fat), 79 g protein, 2,412 mg sodium.
Dietary Exchanges (recipe totals): Bread, 22.5; Fat, 2.66; Fruit, 0; Lean Meat, 2.21; Milk, 1; Vegetables, 0.
Remember to divide totals by the number of servings.

Honey Yogurt Batter Bread

Servings: Makes six to eight servings

White Lily Flour is the only flour my mother would ever use. She always said it baked better cakes and biscuits than any other kind. It is the flour I grew up eating and baking with, and it mixes differently from the average run-of-the-mill flour. It's a soft winter-wheat flour that is pre-sifted, and it's wonderful to work with.

This recipe was printed on the last bag of flour I used, and it's a great bread to bake in a Dutch oven. I've amended it slightly for easier baking on the trail or a boat.

Ingredients	All-Dry
4 cups enriched White Lily white bread flour	4 cups
¼-ounce package rapid-rise yeast	¼-ounce package rapid-rise (or 1 tablespoon)
8 ounces plain whole milk yogurt	⅓ cup powder
¼ cup butter	¼ cup powder
1½ teaspoons salt	1½ teaspoons
¼ cup water	2 cups
⅓ cup honey	⅛ cup powder
1 raw whole egg, extra-large	2 tablespoons powder

Instructions: Combine flour, salt, and yeast in a large bowl. Heat water, yogurt, honey, and butter until warm only. Make a well in the dry ingredients and add the warm mixture. Mix about one cup of the flour mixture with the liquids, then whip the egg into that mixture. Continue mixing dry mixture with egg mixture until all is blended. Pour into a greased Dutch oven. Let rise about thirty minutes then stir down and let rise again until double in bulk. Bake at about 350 degrees for forty to forty-five minutes.

(RECIPE COURTESY OF WHITE LILY FLOUR)

Recipe Totals: 2,975 calories, 504 g carbohydrates (15 g dietary fiber and 109 g sugars), 400 mg cholesterol, 69 g total fat (37 g saturated fat), 84 g protein, 3,864 mg sodium.

Dietary Exchanges (recipe totals): Bread, 0; Fat, 11.2; Fruit, 5.33; Lean Meat, 1.1; Milk, 1; Vegetables, 0.79.

Remember to divide totals by the number of servings.

Jean's English Muffins

Servings: Makes eight to ten muffins

Our family has always enjoyed toasted English Muffins for breakfast as a nice change of pace from toasted bread or biscuits. This recipe makes a relatively small batch and I find that using a heat diffuser over the heat source really helps these muffins to cook without burning. (See the BushBaker discussion on page 16 on how to make your own.)

Ingredients	All-Dry
¼-ounce rapid-rise yeast	¼-ounce package (or 1 tablespoon)
2 teaspoons white granulated sugar	2 teaspoons
3 cups enriched flour	3 cups
2 tablespoons self-rising, enriched white cornmeal	2 tablespoons
½ cup sour cream powder	½ cup
½ teaspoon salt	½ teaspoon
1⅛ cups water	1¾ cups

Instructions: Combine yeast, sugar, and warm water in a large bowl. Gradually mix in flour, salt, and sour cream powder. Turn dough out on a floured board and knead out any bubbles. Let dough rest for five to ten minutes, then roll it out half-an-inch thick. Cut out three-inch diameter muffins and sprinkle them with cornmeal. Let them rise for thirty minutes. Grease skillet lightly with olive oil and heat it on top of a heat diffuser at very low temperature. Carefully place four or five muffins in the skillet, cornmeal side down. Cook each side for ten minutes.

Recipe Totals: 2,203 calories, 338 g carbohydrates (13 g dietary fiber and 15 g sugar), 107 mg cholesterol, 68 g total fat (0.1 g saturated fat), 60 g protein, 1,781 mg sodium.

Dietary Exchanges (recipe totals): Bread, 16.9; Fat, 13.9; Fruit, 0.542; Lean Meat, 0; Milk, 2.27; Vegetables, 0.

Remember to divide totals by the number of servings.

Jean's Pita Bread

Servings: Makes four large pitas

Pita bread is one of the simplest forms of yeast bread. It originated in the Mediterranean, and is a yeasted flat bread. It is easy to make and keeps very well. The oil in this recipe is optional.

Ingredients	All-Dry
3 cups enriched flour	3 cups
2 tablespoons olive oil	2 tablespoons powder
¼-ounce rapid-rise yeast	¼-ounce package (or 1 tablespoon)
4 ounces sour cream powder	½ cup
2 teaspoons white granulated sugar	2 teaspoons
1½ teaspoons salt	1½ teaspoons
1 cup water	1½ cups

Instructions: In a large bowl, combine yeast, sugar, salt, water, and oil. Gradually add flour and sour cream powder. Turn dough out on a floured surface and divide into four pieces. Flatten each piece and roll to about six inches in diameter and one-eighth inch thick. Let dough rest for ten to fifteen minutes. Heat oven to 450 degrees F. Cook for four to six minutes until the pitas have puffed up into a ball. Remove pitas and let cool. To save space, you can flatten the pitas for storage.

Recipe Totals: 2,391 calories, 328 g carbohydrates (12 g dietary fiber and 15 g sugars), 108 mg cholesterol, 94 g total fat (4 g saturated fat), 59 g protein, 3,722 mg sodium.

Dietary Exchanges (recipe totals): Bread, 16.9; Fat, 19.1; Fruit, 0.542; Lean Meat, 0; Milk, 2.27; Vegetables, 0.

Remember to divide totals by the number of servings.

Quick Caraway-Rye Beer Yeast Bread

Servings: Makes one large loaf. Serves four to six.

T his is a wonderful whole-grain bread. If you don't want to mess with a yeast bread while you're hiking or boating, fix this at home when fresh ingredients are available, and enjoy it for the first day of your trip. I love this bread with hot mustard, corned beef, sauerkraut, and Monterey Jack cheese. Just writing about it makes me want to run to the kitchen and fix some up.

Ingredients	All-Dry
2¼ cups enriched flour	2¼ cups
1½ cups medium rye flour	1½ cups
6 fluid ounces beer	nil
2 tablespoons honey	⅛ cup powder
1 tablespoon olive oil	1 tablespoon butter powder
½ ounce rapid-rise yeast	2 tablespoons (2 packages instant)
½ cup water	1½ cups
1 tablespoon caraway seed	1 tablespoon
1½ teaspoons salt	1½ teaspoons
½ ounce garlic salt	2 teaspoons

Instructions: Combine water, beer, honey, and olive oil, and heat moderately. Mix dry ingredients, then gradually blend in honey-beer mixture until it forms a stiff but moist dough. Place on pastry sheet and knead for four minutes, or until smooth. Place dough in an oiled pan and turn it over so that it's completely covered with oil. Cover and let rise for about twenty to thirty-five minutes—until double in bulk. Bake at 375 degrees F for thirty minutes or until done.

Note: When using all-dry ingredients, warm all of the water by itself, then mix as directed above.

Recipe Totals: 1,992 calories, 393 g carbohydrates (35 g dietary fiber and 51 g sugars), 0 g cholesterol, 20 g total fat (2 g saturated fat), 58 g protein, 8,978 mg sodium.
Dietary Exchanges (recipe totals): Bread, 20.2; Fat, 3.33; Fruit, 2; Lean Meat, 0; Milk, 0; Vegetables, 0.
Remember to divide totals by the number of servings.

Li-Xi's Steamed Dumpling Wrapper

Servings: Makes 24 wrappers

This recipe was given to the King Arthur Flour company by Li-Xi (pronounced Lee-Shee), a native of Shanghai, China. These dumplings, or buns, can be served plain, but I've also included instructions for dumplings with fillings. They're wonderful, so be sure to look at the Filled Dumpling recipe.

Ingredients	All-Dry
1½ cups water	1½ cups
1 teaspoon white granulated sugar	1 teaspoon
1 package regular dry yeast	1 tablespoon rapid-rise
1 teaspoon salt	1 teaspoon
4 cups multipurpose white wheat flour	4 cups

Instructions: Pour water into mixing bowl and add yeast and sugar. When yeast mixture is frothy, add the salt and three-and-a-half cups of flour. Mix well. Mixture should pull away from the sides of the bowl. Turn dough out on a lightly floured surface and knead until it's smooth and elastic. Place dough in a greased bowl, cover, and allow to rise until double in bulk. This takes about thirty minutes with rapid-rise yeast and ninety minutes with regular yeast.

Turn dough out on floured surface and punch down. Pinch off large marble-sized pieces of dough. Shape them into small balls, cover them, and let them rise for about twenty minutes. Bring water to a boil in the bottom of your steamer. Place dumplings on the rack over the water, cover, and when the water has come to a boil again, turn the heat down and let the dumplings steam for about thirty minutes.

(RECIPE COURTESY OF KING ARTHUR FLOUR)

Recipe Totals: 3,588 calories, 352 g carbohydrates (55 g dietary fiber and 27 sugars), 1,032 mg cholesterol, 135 g total fat (37 g saturated fat), 266 g protein, 6,937 mg sodium.

Dietary Exchanges (recipe totals): Bread, 0; Fat, 11.6; Fruit, 0.271; Lean Meat, 29.4; Milk, 0; Vegetables, 1.12.

Remember to divide totals by the number of servings.

Li-Xi's Steamed Dumpling with Filling

Servings: Makes twenty-four dumplings. Serves six.

Like the previous recipe, this one was given to King Arthur Flour by Li-Xi. These dumplings, or buns, are best cooked in a Chinese bamboo steamer, although it's possible to rig up a makeshift steamer with a large kettle and something on which to place the dumplings to keep them above the water in the bottom. The BakePacker would be perfect for this. You might try a greased cake rack, or a piece of screening placed on three empty tin cans with their tops and bottoms removed.

Ingredients	All-Dry
(1) Wrapper:	
1½ cups water	1½ cups
1 teaspoon white granulated sugar	1 teaspoon
1 package regular dry yeast	1 tablespoon rapid-rise
1 teaspoon salt	1 teaspoon
4 cups multipurpose white wheat flour	4 cups
(2) Filling:	
1½ pounds lean, roasted pork centerloin	1½ cups freeze-dried
2 raw whole eggs, extra-large	4 tablespoons powder
2 tablespoons soy sauce	1 tablespoon powder
1 teaspoon salt	1 teaspoon
¼ cup peanut oil	¼ cup powder
2 tablespoons ginger root slices	2 tablespoons
1 tablespoon Mirin wine (Japanese)	1 tablespoon powder
nil water	1¾ cups

Instructions: **(1) Wrappers:** Follow the previous recipe instructions for Li-Xi's Steamed Dumpling Wrapper. Turn dough out on floured surface and punch down. Pinch off large marble-size pieces of dough. Then, shape them into flat round cakes with your hand. **(2) Filler:** Blend filling ingredients together. Spoon a small amount of the mix into the middle of each round of dough and fold the wrapper over it like a turnover. Pinch the edges together firmly. Steam for thirty-five to forty minutes.

Incidentally, beef, chicken, or seafood may be substituted for pork. Li-Xi has also made sweet dumplings using minced apple, sugar, and cinnamon. These are delicious with green tea.

(RECIPE COURTESY OF KING ARTHUR FLOUR)

Note: The following nutritional information does not include the data for the dumpling wrappers. You will need to add that to this information.

Recipe Totals: 1,524 calories, 341 g carbohydrates (55 g dietary fiber and 21 g sugars), 0 g cholesterol, 8 g total fat (2 g saturated fat), 62 g protein, 2,152 mg sodium.

Dietary Exchanges (recipe totals): Bread, 0; Fat, 0; Fruit, 0.271; Lean Meat, 0; Milk, 0; Vegetables, 0.79.

Remember to divide totals by the number of servings.

Millet Bread

Servings: Serves five

Millet is a small round grain most commonly associated with birdseed. There is a good reason why birds like millet—it's very nutritious. Millet's protein content is sixteen to twenty-two percent, surpassed only by wheat germ at thirty-six percent and soy at twenty-eight percent. It's used extensively in Mediterranean countries and has become increasingly popular in the United States, mainly at health stores. Give this bread a try. It might just win you over.

Ingredients	All-Dry
1 cup honey	½ cup powder
⅔ cup warm water	⅔ cup
1½ cups cool water	2½ cups
¼-ounce rapid-rise yeast	1 tablespoons
2 cups whole wheat flour	2 cups
1½ teaspoons salt	1½ teaspoons
8 ounces whole-grain foxtail millet	2 cups
5 cups enriched flour	5 cups

Instructions: Combine honey, warm water, and yeast. Set aside. Blend dry ingredients together and then add yeast mixture. The yeast mix should be foaming; if it's not, your yeast is dead and your bread will not rise. Add the cool water. Knead well and divide into five pieces. Make into rounds and let rise for thirty to forty minutes until double in volume. Bake at 375 degrees F for twenty-five to thirty-five minutes.

Recipe Totals: 494 calories, 1,116 g carbohydrates (52 g dietary fiber and 281 g sugars), 0 g cholesterol, 18 g total fat (1 g saturated fat), 131 g protein, 3,268 mg sodium.

Dietary Exchanges (recipe totals): Bread, 47.8; Fat, 0; Fruit, 16; Lean Meat, 0; Milk, 0; Vegetables, 0.

Remember to divide totals by the number of servings.

Sour-Cream Biscuits

Servings: Makes twelve biscuits. Serves six.

These biscuits are a richer variation of what my mother called "angel biscuits." They use a combination of yeast and baking powder. You cook only what you want to use immediately. Unused portions of the dough can be kept in a container in the refrigerator for as long as a week. I guess this was the forerunner of the canned biscuit. It certainly makes a wonderfully light and delicate biscuit.

Ingredients	All-Dry
¼-ounce package rapid-rise yeast	¼-ounce package (or 1 tablespoon)
1 tablespoon white granulated sugar	1 tablespoon
3 cups enriched flour	3 cups
1 teaspoon double-acting baking powder	1 teaspoon
1 teaspoon salt	1 teaspoon
½ cup whole milk	⅙ cup powder
⅓ cup cultured sour cream	¼ cup powder
3 tablespoons butter oil (ghee)	3 tablespoons butter powder
½ cup warm water	1¼ cups

Instructions: Combine yeast, sugar, and warm water. Set aside. Combine all other dry ingredients. Add butter, sour cream, milk, and yeast mixture to dry ingredients. Have a small sack of extra flour, or put about half a cup of flour in a bowl. Spoon the dough out the size you want your biscuits to be. Use only the dough that you want to cook, and place balance in the refrigerator or ice chest. Roll biscuits in flour and shape the dough. Pat biscuits onto a greased baking sheet. Let rise for fifteen to twenty minutes. Bake at 400 degrees F for fifteen to twenty minutes or until tops are lightly browned.

Recipe Totals: 2,014 calories, 317 g carbohydrates (12 g dietary fiber and 28 g sugars), 149 mg cholesterol, 62 g total fat (36 g saturated fat), 50 g protein, 2,736 mg sodium.

Dietary Exchanges (recipe totals): Bread, 16.9; Fat, 9.81; Fruit, 0.813; Lean Meat, 0; Milk, 0.80; Vegetables, 0.

Remember to divide totals by the number of servings.

Whole-Wheat Yeast Rolls

Servings: Makes twelve rolls. Serves six.

Sam and I both love whole-wheat breads and rolls. We like the more solid texture and chewy bite. Fortunately for us, they also have more nutrition and fiber. I like this roll recipe because it is so simple to make. I vary the recipe with half-rolled oats or rye and a quarter-cup of sesame seeds or flax seeds. I think you'll enjoy the ease of preparation.

Ingredients	All-Dry
1 cup warm water	2 cups
½ cup olive oil	½ cup
⅛ cup molasses	1½ tablespoons powder
2 cups enriched flour	2 cups
1½ cups whole-wheat flour	1½ cups
¼ cup white granulated sugar	¼ cup
1 teaspoon salt	1 teaspoon
2 × ¼-ounce packages rapid-rise yeast	2 × ¼-ounce packages (or 2 tablespoons)
1 raw whole egg, extra-large	⅛ cup powder

Instructions: Combine warm water, yeast, and white sugar. Set aside. Mix flours and salt. Begin adding yeast mixture to the flour mixture. Halfway through the mixing, add egg, olive oil, and molasses to flour mixture, then continue adding yeast mixture to form dough. Let rise for about thirty minutes, then pinch dough off and roll between hands to shape. Bake at 375 degrees F for fifteen to twenty minutes.

Note: If you're not using rapid-rise yeast, let the dough rise until double in bulk before baking.

Recipe Totals: 2,896 calories, 408 g carbohydrates (29 g dietary fiber and 83 g sugars), 247 mg cholesterol, 120 g total fat (17 g saturated fat), 63 g protein, 2,244 mg sodium.
Dietary Exchanges (recipe totals): Bread, 18.8; Fat, 21.5; Fruit, 5.3; Lean Meat, 1.1; Milk, 0; Vegetables, 0.
Remember to divide totals by the number of servings.

WILD-YEAST (SOURDOUGH) BREADS

I used to think all yeasts were pretty much the same in their reaction to their foodstuffs and environment. But that's not true. Wild yeasts vary considerably in their reactions, and some are much more delicate than regular commercial baker's yeast.

I've read many books about sourdough and I've concluded there are as many wild-yeast philosophies as there are books. I find it doesn't pay to worry too much about growing your own wild yeast. In fact, my attitude is very relaxed after the first three or four weeks of growing the starter. Initially, I feed the starter according to the recipe schedule and I remain diligent for a minimum of three weeks, after which I work out my own schedule. Usually I cut the regular schedule in half, so if I've been feeding the starter every day for the first three weeks, I feed it every other day for the next three weeks, and so on until I can feed it once a week.

Not all sourdough starters will survive this harsh regime, but it suits my lifestyle and the frequency of my bread baking. A starter can quickly increase in size if you don't bake every day, but one that's able to conform to my schedule is more easily kept under control. After trying a few starters, you'll be able to decide for yourself whether you simply want to follow the recipe directions or experiment with controlling the rate of growth.

Potato Malt Starter

This is a cross between Joanne's Sourdough Starter and the California Sourdough Starter. Feed this starter every other day with one cup water with three tablespoons of instant potato granules or flakes added to it, and one cup of malted bread flour. About every other week, add half a cup of sugar to the feeding.

Ingredients

4 cups bread flour
2 teaspoons salt
2 tablespoons white granulated sugar
6 tablespoons dried mashed potatoes, granules or flakes
4 cups water

Instructions: Combine all ingredients and cover loosely with cheese cloth. If you use a plastic container do not screw the lid on tightly or the container could rupture from the pressure of gas. The container should be only half full. Let this mixture stand for five days before you begin feeding it. At the end of five days, bubbles should be working to the surface of the mixture and it should have a slightly sweet fermented smell. It is now ready for use and should be fed every second day.

Recipe Totals: 755 calories, 144 g carbohydrates (11 g dietary fiber and 26 g sugars), 9 mg cholesterol, 13 g total fat (4 g saturated fat), 19 g protein, 5,399 mg sodium.

Dietary Exchanges (recipe totals): Bread, 8.3; Fat, 0; Fruit, 1.63; Lean Meat, 0; Milk, 0; Vegetables, 0.

Remember to divide totals by the number of servings.

California Sourdough Starter

This makes an excellent starter. When selecting grapes, use only those that have been organically grown. You'll find them at health-food stores. As the skin of the grapes is the source of the wild yeast, you should wash the grapes as little as possible, if at all. If you don't use organically grown grapes, and the growers have used pesticides, you will risk contamination of your starter. I have some of organic grape starter in my kitchen right now. It has a wonderful mellow flavor that is quite unlike my potato sourdough starter (Joanne's Starter), which I also love.

Ingredients

½ cup Tokay, Empress, or Red Fame grapes
1 cup enriched bread flour
1 cup whole milk

Instructions: Using warm milk, combine the ingredients in a glass or plastic container that has been sterilized to avoid introducing foreign organisms that might also feed on the starter mixture. Your container should be about three times larger than the amount of starter. Let the starter stand covered at room temperature for seven to twelve days. Stir once a day and distribute the yeast evenly so it can feed and grow. After ten days it should be nice and bubbly, and it should have a slightly sweet fermented smell. It is now ready to use, and you should begin regular feedings once a day of half a cup of bread flour and half a cup of water or white grape juice.

Note: If you don't like the idea of grapes floating in your starter, put them in a cheesecloth and tie it with cotton string. Before adding the grapes to the mixture, mash them with a potato masher and then add them to mixture, juice and all. The cheesecloth and grape residue should be removed after four weeks.

Recipe Totals: 278 calories, 39 g carbohydrates (1 g dietary fiber and 26 g sugars), 33 mg cholesterol, 9 g total fat (5 g saturated fat), 11 g protein, 123 mg sodium.
Dietary Exchanges (recipe totals): Bread, 0.9; Fat, 1.5; Fruit, 1; Lean Meat, 0; Milk, 1; Vegetables, 0.
Remember to divide totals by the number of servings.

California Sourdough Bread

Servings: Makes two large loaves. Serves six.

California Sourdough Bread is wonderful. I have been told that some commercial bakeries keep their sourdough under lock and key to protect their investment. It is, after all, their particular sourdough starter that gives their bread its special flavor.

The differences between one sourdough starter and another can be vast. Even starters made from the same recipe will have differences in growth, flavor tenacity, and longevity. The sheer variety of flavors, and the textures that can be achieved, are what keep folks so interested in baking sourdough bread.

I think you will enjoy this mixture. I have made sourdough batters without sugar and I find that while they work well, they occasionally get too sour for my taste. That's when I add extra sugar to my starter. White grape juice, instead of water, will do the trick, too. Don't be afraid to try something new. I'm always experimenting.

Ingredients	All-Dry
1 cup California Sourdough Starter (See previous recipe)	1 cup (no dry version)
⅓ cup white granulated sugar	⅓ cup
½ cup olive oil	¼ cup shortening powder
1 tablespoon salt	1 tablespoon
1½ cups water	2 cups
6 cups bread flour, enriched	6 cups

Instructions: Start your bread late in the day because it will need at least twelve to eighteen hours to rise. Combine California Sourdough Starter with room-temperature water, sugar, flour, olive oil, and salt. Knead well and use a little more olive oil to coat the outside of the bread dough lightly. Allow to rise overnight in a bread pan (a skillet will work fine if you are backpacking, and making only about a quarter of the recipe). Wrap or cover the top of the pan with cheesecloth or a towel and add a blanket if it is cold or drafty, to keep the yeast from getting too cold. You might even want to keep it in your tent—but only if you are in an area where there are no bears. By next morning, your bread should have doubled in bulk. At this point, if you are at home, punch it down and let it rise for another twelve hours. If you're backpacking, I suggest you go ahead and cook it after one rising period.

Recipe Totals: 1,826 calories, 178 g carbohydrates (4 g dietary fiber and 86 g sugars), 22 mg cholesterol, 117 g total fat (19 g saturated fat), 22 g protein, 6,497 mg sodium.

Dietary Exchanges (recipe totals): Bread, 5.99; Fat, 21.9; Fruit, 4.99; Lean Meat, 0; Milk, 0.659; Vegetables, 0.

Remember to divide totals by the number of servings.

Joanne's Potato Sourdough Starter

This is the recipe for my niece Joanne's sourdough starter. It is truly different from any sourdough starter I've ever used in the past. They've all had flour in them. It has a semi-sweet smell that is pleasant, and none of the sour flavor that I associate with true sourdough. It makes a wonderful, distinctive loaf. I think you'll enjoy it.

Ingredients	All-Dry
1 tablespoon dehydrated potato flakes	1 tablespoon
¾ cup white granulated sugar	¾ cup
1 cup water	1 cup
¼-ounce package regular dry yeast	1 tablespoon

Instructions: This is the recipe to begin a new starter. Mix ingredients in a sterilized jar or non-metallic container and leave for three to five days, by which time the mixture should be bubbling. You can now store your starter in a jar or jug in the refrigerator. Every week, you will need to feed your starter using the ingredients listed above, with the exception of yeast. Each time you feed your starter, remove it from the refrigerator and let it work at room temperature for a night. Incidentally, if your starter ever fails, and your dough doesn't rise, add a fresh, quarter-ounce package of regular dry yeast the next time you feed it.

Recipe Totals: 613 calories, 155 g carbohydrates (2 g dietary fiber and 150 g sugars), 0 g cholesterol, 0.4 g total fat (0 g saturated fat), 3 g protein, 8 mg sodium.
Dietary Exchanges (recipe totals): Bread, 0.125; Fat, 0; Fruit, 9.75; Lean Meat, 0; Milk, 0; Vegetables, 0.85.
Remember to divide totals by the number of servings.

Joanne's Potato Sourdough Bread

Servings: Makes three loaves. Serves six to eight.

Joanne is a niece of mine, my oldest sister's daughter. I spent almost as much time at Sister and Arthur's house with Joanne, Linda, and James when I was growing up as I did at home. Joanne and I have always been close friends and enjoy sharing recipes and cooking. Joanne started baking bread using the sourdough starter described above. Everyone loved the bread so much that she now has lots of regular customers and happy neighbors. Linda also likes to cook, and makes biscuits for a catering service in Atlanta.

Special note: Sourdough yeast grows more slowly than regular baker's yeast, so the dough needs a day-and-a-half of rising before it's ready to bake. Work out your schedule and plan accordingly.

Ingredients	All-Dry
1 cup Joanne's Potato Sourdough Starter	1 cup (no dry version)
1 teaspoon salt	1 teaspoon
⅔ cup white granulated sugar	⅔ cup
½ cup olive oil	⅓ cup shortening powder
6 cups enriched bread flour	6 cups
1½ cups water	2 cups

Instructions: In a large bowl, combine starter, sugar, olive oil, salt, and water. Gradually add flour and blend well. Put in a greased bowl and let rise for twelve to fifteen hours. Note that if the bread has not at least doubled in bulk after the first rising, something is wrong with your starter. It is prudent to keep rapid rise yeast on hand, and I would suggest that you go ahead and add one quarter-ounce package of rapid-rise yeast dissolved in a little warm water with a teaspoon of sugar. Make a depression in the dough and add the yeast mixture. With your hands, thoroughly mix the yeast into the dough. If the dough becomes sticky, mix in a dusting of more flour. Allow the dough to double in bulk, about an hour. This will insure that your bread will rise. (Sometimes I use the sourdough starter and rapid-rise yeast intentionally; I like the flavor of the bread it produces.)

Turn dough out onto a floured work surface, knead, and divide into three loaves. Put in oiled loaf pans and leave to rise for eight to ten hours or until it has doubled in bulk. Bake at 350 degrees F for forty to forty-five minutes.

Recipe Totals: 2,260 calories, 307 g carbohydrates (4 g dietary fiber and 221 g sugars), 11 mg cholesterol, 112 g total fat (15 g saturated fat), 17 g protein, 2,147 mg sodium.

Dietary Exchanges (recipe totals): Bread, 5.47; Fat, 21; Fruit, 14.2; Lean Meat, 0; Milk, 0; Vegetables, 0.485.

Remember to divide totals by the number of servings.

Sourdough Starter No. 1

This starter recipe comes from Mrs. Arthur D. Miles of the Lazy AM Ranch in Bozeman, Montana. It's taken from *The Cowboy Cookbook*, by the Society for Range Management.

Mrs. Miles says: "The ranch is between Livingston and Bozeman, about sixty miles from Yellowstone Park. There was a stopover place here (saloon/post office) where fresh horses were put on stagecoaches going over Bozeman Pass. You can bet lots of sourdough pancakes were served. We still live in the original house, built in 1870."

(RECIPE COURTESY OF THE SOCIETY FOR RANGE MANAGEMENT)

Ingredients

½ tablespoon regular dry yeast
2½ cups warm water
1 tablespoon white granulated sugar
2 cups enriched flour

Instructions: Dissolve yeast in half a cup of water. Add the rest of the ingredients, including the rest of the water, and mix well. Let stand in a covered non-metallic bowl or crock for three days at 76 to 86 degrees F. Stir thoroughly every day. Refrigerate after three days.

(see next page for recipe nutritional data)

Recipe Totals: 952 calories, 206 g carbohydrates (9 g dietary fiber and 17 g sugars), 0 g cholesterol, 3 g total fat (0 g saturated fat), 26 g protein, 2 mg sodium.
Dietary Exchanges (recipe totals): Bread, 11.3; Fat, 0; Fruit, 0.81; Lean Meat, 0; Milk, 0; Vegetables, 0.42.
Remember to divide totals by the number of servings.

Sourdough Pancakes

Servings: Makes eight large pancakes. Serves four.

This recipe is a natural follow-up to Mrs. A. Miles's sourdough starter recipe in *The Cowboy Cookbook*, by the Society for Range Management.

Ingredients	All-Dry
1 cup Sourdough Starter No. 1 (See previous recipe)	1 cup
2 cups water	2½ cups
2½ cups enriched flour	2½ cups
3 tablespoons white granulated sugar	3 tablespoons
1 raw whole egg, extra-large	2 tablespoons egg powder
2 tablespoons olive oil	1 tablespoon shortening powder
1 teaspoon baking soda	1 teaspoon
¼ cup evaporated whole milk, canned	¼ cup milk powder

Instructions: Put starter in a large bowl. Add water, flour, and sugar. Mix well—it will be thick and lumpy. Cover and leave in a warm place overnight. Next morning, take one or two cups of the batter and put it back in the starter bowl. Then, to the remaining batter add egg, cooking oil, milk, salt, baking soda, and sugar. Mix into batter gently. This causes foaming and rising action. Let stand a few minutes and then fry on a hot, greased griddle. Add extra milk if it is too thick. Yummy! Enjoy!

(RECIPE COURTESY OF THE SOCIETY FOR RANGE MANAGEMENT)

Recipe Totals: 1,922 calories, 340 g carbohydrates (13 g dietary fiber and 54 g sugars), 266 mg cholesterol, 41 g total fat (8 g saturated fat), 50 g protein, 1,402 mg sodium.
Dietary Exchanges (recipe totals): Bread, 17; Fat, 6.69; Fruit, 2.65; Lean Meat, 1.1; Milk, 0.5; Vegetables, 0.112.
Remember to divide totals by the number of servings.

Sourdough Bread No. 2

Servings: Makes one large loaf. Serves four.

This recipe is another one that requires you to grow a sponge (a yeast starter) overnight. It's a very good mixture and I think you'll like it. The recipe was given to me by a woman in Bryson City, North Carolina, along with my first cup of starter and a loaf of wonderful bread. The recipe is divided into two parts, first the starter mix and then the bread mix. I hope you enjoy it as much as I have.

Ingredients

(1) **Starter Mix**
1 cup Potato Malt Starter (See page 52)
1 cup bread flour, enriched
1 cup water
¼ cup white granulated sugar

Instructions: Combine the ingredients and let the mixture stand overnight. By morning, the mixture should have doubled in bulk and be frothy.

Ingredients	All-Dry
(2) **Bread Mix**	
4 cups bread flour, enriched	4 cups
1 teaspoon salt	1 teaspoon
1 cup water	1 cup
¼ cup olive oil	¼-cup shortening powder

Instructions: Combine ingredients with matured starter mixture and knead well. Place in an oiled bread pan and let rise for about twelve hours until double in bulk. Bake.

Note: I find that bread flour that has barley malt in it works better than regular flour.

Recipe Totals: 1,141 calories, 142 g carbohydrates (4 g dietary fiber and 56 g sugars), 1 mg cholesterol, 59 g total fat (8 g saturated fat), 15 g protein, 2,952 mg sodium.
Dietary Exchanges (recipe totals): Bread, 5.73; Fat, 10.5; Fruit, 3.49; Lean Meat, 0; Milk, 0; Vegetables, 0.
Remember to divide totals by the number of servings.

Chuck Wagon Chow

❖   ❖   ❖

The great era of cattle-driving across the Texas plains to Kansas railheads lasted only 20 years (approximately from 1865 to 1885), but enough folklore, books, songs, and movies have come out to make it seem like major American history. There are people all over the world who couldn't tell you who John Adams or Thomas Jefferson were, but who know all about Wild Bill Hickock. Millions who can't speak English know the meaning of the words "cowpuncher," "trail boss," and "chuck wagon."

The cattle drives of the West were by no means the first in this country. As early as the 1790s, herds were being driven from western New York and Pennsylvania or along the Cumberland Road to New York City, Baltimore, and Richmond to be slaughtered for meat. And even before that, butchers used to drive cattle from farm to farm, trading beef-on-the-hoof or their services as slaughterers in return for farm produce. On one occasion, during the 1850s, some enterprising Texans drove 150 head of cattle all the way to New York. The cattle drive took two years, but the profit was substantial enough to justify the trouble.

Then in 1867, the Kansas and Pacific Railroad reached Abilene, Kansas, and cattle could be shipped to Chicago slaughterhouses, instead of driven on the hoof. Later, as the rails moved westward, other towns in Kansas—notably Dodge City—took over from Abilene as the wild "cow towns."

Although the cowboys took their orders from the trail boss, the cook was the real keeper of the crew. Besides preparing three hot meals a day, he also served as doctor and barber.

On starlit nights his last responsibility before turning in was to point the chuck wagon's tongue toward the North star so the trail boss would have a sure compass heading the next morning.

The dining table on the range was anything the cowboy found usable. He used the ground, his lap, or his bedroll as a table. No one was allowed to use the cook's private workbench. The cowhand picked out his utensils, and then went from pot to pot helping himself to food and coffee. He took all he could eat at his first helping—just in case there wasn't enough for a second helping. Usually the cowboy was considerate of others, following a strict etiquette. When removing the lid from a pot for a helping, he was careful to place it so the lid wouldn't touch sand. Then he stood downwind so that any dust he kicked up wouldn't blow into someone's food. He never took the last pieces of food unless he was sure everyone was finished. It was against the rules to begin dishing up food until the cook called. It was also against custom to ride a horse into camp and tie it to the chuck wagon—no one liked horse hair in their food. If a cowboy refilled his coffee cup and another hand called "man the pot," he was obliged to go around and fill any cups held out to him. Proper conduct around the wagon was as important to the cowboy as society etiquette was to his Eastern brother.

(From the *Trail Boss's Cowboy Cookbook*, courtesy of the Society for Range Management)

* CHAPTER 4 *
Quick Breads

Quick breads as we know them (biscuits, muffins, scones, and so on) have been around only for the past century. When baking powder was invented, it speeded up the process of making bread but it didn't replace the slower-working yeast altogether because yeast breads have a different taste and texture.

Each quick bread has a distinctive taste and texture that varies with the variety of flour and baking powder.

Today many commercial varieties of baking powder are available, but you can make your own single-acting baking powder by mixing two teaspoonfuls of cream of tartar with one teaspoonful of baking soda. This mixture yields one tablespoon of baking powder. Because this single-action mixture acts quickly, add it at the very last stage of mixing, and do not beat vigorously after its addition. Your mixture should be baked as soon as possible after the addition of baking powder to be sure it will rise. As the name indicates, the mixture will rise only once, so handle carefully and don't stir. Double-acting baking powder can be stirred or beaten and its dough will rise in the oven.

Note that there is a difference between baking powder and baking soda. Baking soda is simply sodium bicarbonate, otherwise known as bicarbonate of soda. Baking powder is baking soda with other ingredients added. If you choose to use baking soda instead of baking powder, you must have an acidic ingredient to react with the soda. This reaction produces the carbon dioxide gas necessary for rising. The most common acidic ingredients used are cream of tartar, buttermilk, natural cocoa powder (non-Dutch or alkalized), yogurt, fruit juice, and sour milk. Honey and molasses will also work.

The general rule of thumb for quantities is one teaspoon of baking powder for each cup of flour. I have a tendency to use only about one half to two-thirds of that amount because I find that too much baking powder or soda can adversely affect the flavor of your baked items. You will have to determine this according to your own taste, of course, by tasting your bread and deciding whether it rose as much as you wanted it to.

Because quick breads generally cook quickly, and require no rising period before baking, they are ideal for boat and trail baking.

BISCUIT AND PANCAKE BREADS

Bacon-Cheese Oven Pancake

Servings: Makes four to six servings.

This is a good way to prepare a hearty breakfast without standing in the galley all morning, or without using all of your fuel for the trail on one meal. It is also a nice change of pace from the regular breakfast routine and works equally well for an easy dinner.

Ingredients	**All-Dry**
12 ounces biscuit mix	2 cups
1 cup Swiss cheese, shredded	⅔ cup dried
½ cup Swiss cheese, shredded	⅓ cup dried
¾ cup whole milk	¼ cup powder
¼ cup maple syrup	¾ cup dry crystals
1 tablespoon white granulated sugar	1 tablespoon
1 raw whole egg, extra large	2 tablespoons powder
12 pieces bacon, cooked	½ cup dried or ¼ cup soy bacos
nil water	1¾ cups

Instructions: Reserve maple syrup, bacon, and the half-cup of cheese for topping. Combine biscuit mix, milk, and egg. Add remaining ingredients and mix well. Pour into a buttered skillet or pan. Top with cheese and bacon. Bake uncovered for ten to fifteen minutes at 375 degrees F. Serve with maple syrup.

Note: When you're using all-dry ingredients, the maple syrup will need to be reconstituted with a quarter-cup of boiling water. Another option is to sprinkle the dry maple on with the cheese and bacon topping before baking. It is great either way.

Recipe Totals: 2,902 calories, 289 g carbohydrates (0 g dietary fiber and 79 g sugars), 64 mg cholesterol, 145 g total fat (61 g saturated fat), 110 g protein, 6,063 mg sodium.

Dietary Exchanges (recipe totals): Bread, 0; Fat, 13.4; Fruit, 3.81; Lean Meat, 10.6; Milk, 0.75; Vegetables, 0.

Remember to divide totals by the number of servings.

Buttermilk Cornbread

Servings: Makes four to six servings.

What could be more satisfying than a chunk of hot buttered cornbread and a bowl of beans with home-grown tomato and Vidalia sweet onion chopped on top? Or the Cajun version, with red beans, rice, and maybe smoked sausage on the side? There's certainly nothing fancy about it, but it could rival almost any other meal. I call it comfort food—food whose flavors bring back memories of momma's cooking, home, and the past.

Ingredients	All-Dry
1 cup enriched flour	1 cup
½ cup self-rising, enriched white cornmeal	½ cup
½ teaspoon salt	½ teaspoon
1 tablespoon double-acting baking powder	1 tablespoon
¼ cup olive oil	¼ cup butter powder
⅓ cup white granulated sugar	⅓ cup
1 raw whole egg, extra-large	2 tablespoons powder
½ cup whole milk	⅛ cup powder
½ cup buttermilk, cultured	¼ cup powder
nil water	1½ cups

Instructions: Combine sugar, egg, and olive oil. Add cornmeal, flour, baking powder, and salt. Add milk and buttermilk and beat until smooth. Pour into a hot, greased skillet and bake for twenty-five minutes at 400 degrees F.

Recipe Totals: 1,604 calories, 222 carbohydrates (8 g dietary fiber and 82 g sugars), 268 mg cholesterol, 68 g total fat (13 g saturated fat), 33 g protein, 3,554 mg sodium.

Dietary Exchanges (recipe totals): Bread, 5.63; Fat, 11.8; Fruit, 4.33; Lean Meat, 1.1; Milk, 1.05; Vegetables, 0.

Remember to divide totals by the number of servings.

Cheddar Cornmeal Cracker

Servings: Makes about three dozen crackers. Serves six.

This recipe was given to King Arthur Flour by Ken Haedrich, who describes himself as "an enthusiastic baker, teacher, food writer, husband, and father." His enthusiasm has found its way into a number of magazines, books, and everything he bakes. As he said in an article he wrote about crackers several years ago, "I enjoy my small role as a cracker revivalist. I see myself as helping to preserve an all-but-forgotten kitchen craft. Making crackers is just good fun, a nice way to unwind after a hectic day, a nice way to spend time with your kids." Ken and his family play and bake in their kitchen in New Hampshire.

Ingredients	All-Dry
1 cup multipurpose white wheat flour	1 cup
¾ cup whole-grain yellow cornmeal	¾ cup
¼ cup whole wheat flour	¼ cup
¼ teaspoon double-acting baking powder	¼ teaspoon
½ teaspoon salt	½ teaspoon
¼ teaspoon red cayenne pepper	¼ teaspoon
1 cup shredded Colby cheese	⅔ cup freeze-dried
1 raw whole egg, extra-large	2 tablespoons powder
¼ cup olive oil	¼ cup shortening powder
¼ cup water	1 cup

Instructions: Combine the flours, cornmeal, baking powder, salt, and cayenne and toss with your hands or a fork. Add the grated cheese and mix again. Make a well depression in the dry ingredients and put in the egg, olive oil, and water. Beat the ingredients in the well together first, then gradually mix in more and more of the dry ingredients until all sticks together. Turn dough out on a floured work surface and roll to about one-eighth of an inch thick. Cut and transfer to an ungreased baking sheet. Bake for about fifteen minutes. They should be crisp and golden when done.

Note: These can be baked in your skillet on low heat using a heat diffuser. Brown on both sides, turning often.

(RECIPE COURTESY OF KING ARTHUR FLOUR)

Recipe Totals: 1,816 calories, 180 g carbohydrates (23 g dietary fiber and 9 g sugars), 354 mg cholesterol, 102 g total fat (33 g saturated fat), 61 g protein, 1,982 mg sodium.

Dietary Exchanges (recipe totals): Bread, 5; Fat, 16.4; Fruit, 0; Lean Meat, 4.83; Milk, 0; Vegetables, 0.

Remember to divide totals by the number of servings.

Cheese and Onion Bread

Servings: Makes four to six servings.

This bread is a little different, since it has the cheese and onion baked on top. I like it with mozzarella cheese and a cup of beef bouillon—it's like having French onion soup, only easier to eat.

Ingredients	All-Dry
3 tablespoons butter oil (ghee)	3 tablespoons shortening powder
1½ cups stir-fried chopped onions	½ cup dried
2 cups enriched flour	2 cups
3 teaspoons double-acting baking powder	3 teaspoons
¹⁄₁₀ ounce dehydrated parsley	2 tablespoons
1 teaspoon salt	1 teaspoon
½ cup shredded Cheddar cheese	½ cup freeze-dried
⅓ cup butter oil (ghee)	⅓ cup shortening powder
1 raw whole egg, extra-large	2 tablespoons powder
1 cup whole milk	⅓ cup powder
nil water	2⅔ cups

Instructions: Sauté onion in three tablespoons butter. Reserve one cup sautéed onion and cheese for topping. Mix all of the ingredients together until well blended. Pour in a buttered pan and top with reserved onions and cheese. Bake at 425 degrees F for thirty minutes.

Recipe Totals: 2,426 calories, 238 g carbohydrates (14 g dietary fiber and 37 g sugars), 613 mg cholesterol, 142 g total fat (85 g saturated fat), 59 g protein, 4,161 mg sodium.

Dietary Exchanges (recipe totals): Bread, 11.3; Fat, 21.4; Fruit, 0; Lean Meat, 3.08; Milk, 1; Vegetables, 4.85.

Remember to divide totals by the number of servings.

Baked Corn Spoon Bread

Servings: Makes eight servings.

There are so many things you can do with this bread. You can serve it as a bread or use it as a base for chili, tacos, or barbecue. Serve it with beef stew, chicken à la king, or pinto beans topped with onions. No matter how you serve it, you'll love it if you like spoon bread or polenta.

Ingredients	All-Dry
16 ounces creamed white corn, canned, not drained	1½ cups freeze-dried
16 ounces yellow corn, canned, not drained	1½ cups freeze-dried
8 ounces cream cheese	⅔ cup powder
¼ cup butter oil (ghee)	¼ cup powder
8 ounces sweet muffin mix, dry	2 cups (1 small box)
1 raw whole egg, extra-large	2 tablespoons dried
nil water	3 cups

Instructions: Combine cream cheese, butter and corn muffin mix. Blend well. Add all other ingredients and pour into a buttered skillet. Bake at 375 degrees F for thirty-five minutes.

Recipe Totals: 2,858 calories, 318 g carbohydrates (9 g dietary fiber and 32 g sugars), 628 mg cholesterol, 165 g total fat (84 g saturated fat), 53 protein, 4,547 mg sodium.

Dietary Exchanges (recipe totals): Bread, 12.2; Fat, 27.9; Fruit, 6.03; Lean Meat, 3.37; Milk, 0; Vegetables, 0.

Remember to divide totals by the number of servings.

Cheesy Garlic Biscuits

Servings: Makes nine to twelve biscuits. Serves six.

These biscuits are good with just about everything. I've had similar ones in seafood restaurants. You probably have too.

Ingredients	All-Dry
2 cups biscuit mix	2 cups
⅔ cup whole milk	¼ cup powder
½ cup shredded Cheddar cheese	⅓ cup freeze-dried
½ teaspoon parsley flakes	½ teaspoon
1 teaspoon garlic powder	1 teaspoon
nil water	¾ cup

Instructions: Combine all ingredients and mix well. Roll out and cut into biscuits. As an option, you may brush the top with melted butter and sprinkle with more garlic and parsley. Bake at 400 degrees F for ten to twelve minutes, or until brown.

(see next page for recipe nutritional data)

Recipe Totals: 1,740 calories, 219 g carbohydrates (0.6 g dietary fiber and 9 g sugars), 81 mg cholesterol, 75 g total fat (29 g saturated fat), 48 g protein, 4,699 mg sodium.
Dietary Exchanges (recipe totals): Bread, 1.98; Fat, 3.68; Fruit, 0; Lean Meat, 0; Milk, 0.667; Vegetables, 0.
Remember to divide totals by the number of servings.

Cheese Puff Casserole Bread

Servings: Makes two to four servings.

This bread is a little more time-consuming to make than most, and it does require whipped egg whites. It will probably be one of those recipes you will want to fix at home, but once you have tried it, you will understand why I didn't want to leave it out of the book.

Ingredients	All-Dry
¼ cup butter oil (ghee)	¼ cup shortening powder
¼ cup enriched flour	¼ cup
1 cup whole milk	⅓ cup powder
¼ cup shredded Cheddar cheese	3 tablespoons
2 raw whole eggs, extra-large	4 tablespoons powder
1 egg white	2 tablespoons powder
nil water	1½ cups

Instructions: Place butter and flour in a skillet and cook for about one minute. Add milk and stir until thick, remove from heat. Let cool slightly and add cheese. Beat egg yolk and add to mixture. Whip egg white and fold into batter. Pour into a greased deep dish or pan and bake for fifty minutes at 325 degrees F, or until done.

Note: If using all-dry ingredients, make a paste with shortening powder and flour. Mix milk powder with one cup of water and gradually stir into flour paste then cook until thick. Add a quarter-cup water to egg powder and mix until smooth, then add to mixture. Add a quarter-cup of water to egg whites and whip. Fold into batter and cook as directed above.

Recipe Totals: 997 calories, 37 g carbohydrates (1 g dietary fiber and 14 g sugars), 688 mg cholesterol, 80 g total fat (46 g saturated fat), 33 g protein, 442 mg sodium.
Dietary Exchanges (recipe totals): Bread, 1.41; Fat, 12; Fruit, 0; Lean Meat, 3.2; Milk, 1; Vegetables, 0.
Remember to divide totals by the number of servings.

Cheesy Spinach Muffins

Servings: Makes twelve muffins. Serves six.

This is really a whole meal in muffin form. It's great to bake while you are eating your breakfast, and then you have your lunch ready also.

Ingredients	All-Dry
⅔ cup whole milk	¼ cup dried milk
1 tablespoon olive oil	1 tablespoon shortening powder
½ cup raw chopped spinach	¼ cup dehydrated
3 raw whole eggs, extra-large	6 tablespoons powder
½ cup shredded Swiss cheese	⅓ cup freeze-dried
2 tablespoons chopped spring/green onions	1 tablespoon freeze-dried
¼ cup grated Parmesan cheese	¼ cup
2 cups biscuit mix	2 cups
nil water	1¾ cups water

Instructions: Combine biscuit mix, cheeses, onions, olive oil, and eggs. Gradually mix in milk. When blended, fold in spinach. Bake in greased skillet, or spoon into muffin cups and bake at 350 degrees F for thirty minutes.

Recipe Totals: 2,204 calories, 222 g carbohydrates (1 g dietary fiber and 13 g sugars), 833 mg cholesterol, 110 g total fat (39 g saturated fat), 81 g protein, 5,188 mg sodium.

Dietary Exchanges (recipe totals): Bread, 0; Fat, 8; Fruit, 0; Lean Meat, 6.95; Milk, 0.667; Vegetables, 0.374.

Remember to divide totals by the number of servings.

Cheese Spoon Bread

Servings: Makes six servings.

If you like cornbread but have never had spoon bread, you are in for a treat. To me, it's a cross between cornbread and polenta. It has a smoother texture than cornbread, and a lighter texture than polenta. If I have left-over spoon bread, I like to dip it in a beaten egg and fry it for breakfast like you would French toast. Yum!

(continued)

Ingredients	All-Dry
1 cup whole-grain yellow cornmeal	1 cup
1 teaspoon salt	1 teaspoon
2 tablespoons butter oil (ghee)	2 tablespoons shortening powder
1½ cups shredded Cheddar cheese	1 cup freeze-dried
1 cup whole milk	⅓ cup powder
3 raw whole eggs, extra-large	6 tablespoons powder
¼ teaspoon red Cayenne pepper	¼ teaspoon
1 teaspoon double-acting baking powder	1 teaspoon
2 cups water	3½ cups

Instructions: Whip eggs and milk together. Add cornmeal, butter, salt, and baking powder. Next, add water, pepper, and cheese. Bake in a greased deep dish or Dutch oven for fifty to sixty minutes at 375 degrees F.

Note: If using all-dry ingredients, gradually add water to dry blend for a smoother batter before pouring into a greased baking dish.

Recipe Totals: 1,762 calories, 111 g carbohydrates (9 g dietary fiber and 16 g sugars), 1,018 mg cholesterol, 112 g total fat (63 g saturated fat), 82 g protein, 4,055 mg sodium.

Dietary Exchanges (recipe totals): Bread, 5; Fat, 15.3; Fruit, 0; Lean Meat, 9.25; Milk, 1; Vegetables, 0.

Remember to divide totals by the number of servings.

Complete Meal Muffins

Servings: Makes four to six servings.

These muffins really are a complete meal. Bake them for a very satisfying entreé at any meal.

Ingredients	All-Dry
2 cups canned corned beef	2 cups freeze-dried beef
2 cups soft bread crumbs	2 cups croutons
2 raw whole eggs, extra-large	4 tablespoons powder
2 tablespoons packed brown sugar	2 tablespoons
1 tablespoon mustard powder	1 tablespoon
2 tablespoons water	2 cups

Instructions: Combine all ingredients and bake in greased muffin tins at 300 degrees F for thirty-five minutes.

Recipe Totals: 1,452 calories, 76 g carbohydrates (2 g dietary fiber and 33 g sugars), 789 mg cholesterol, 71 g total fat (25 g saturated fat), 119 g protein, 4,035 mg sodium.
Dietary Exchanges (recipe totals): Bread, 3.03; Fat, 4.16; Fruit, 1.71; Lean Meat, 15.2; Milk, 0; Vegetables, 0.
Remember to divide totals by the number of servings.

Chili Cheese Biscuits

Servings: Makes four biscuits. Serves two to three.

This is great with Mexican food, chili, or just a bowl of pinto beans with salsa on top. In the South, we would say that's "Mighty fine eatin'."

Ingredients	All-Dry
1 cup all-purpose enriched white flour	1 cup
1 tablespoon double-acting baking powder	1 tablespoon
½ teaspoon salt	½ teaspoon
¼ cup canola oil	⅛ cup shortening powder
½ cup 2 percent low-fat milk with vitamin A	⅛ cup milk powder
1 teaspoon chili powder or taco seasoning	1 teaspoon
¼ cup shredded Cheddar cheese	¼ cup freeze-dried
nil water	¾ cup

Instructions: Combine all dry ingredients. Add oil to milk and gradually mix with dry ingredients to form dough. Bake at 400 degrees F for fifteen to twenty minutes or until golden brown.
Note: Packaged chili cheese-dip mix may also be used in place of the chili powder and Cheddar cheese. But be aware that the following nutritional data is not valid for packaged dip mix.

Recipe Totals: 1,121 calories, 104 g carbohydrates (5 g dietary fiber and 9 g sugars), 39 mg cholesterol, 68 g total fat (12 g saturated fat), 24 g protein, 1,019 mg sodium.
Dietary Exchanges (recipe totals): Bread, 5.66; Fat, 12.5; Fruit, 0; Lean Meat, 0.989; Milk, 0.5; Vegetables, 0.333.
Remember to divide totals by the number of servings.

Crepes (Very Thin Pancakes)

Servings: Makes 16 crepes. Serves four to six.

When I was in college, I knew a couple from London, England. Once, after dinner, we were craving dessert and she whipped up some crepes for us. It was just a simple thing, but it seemed so elegant and special. After she fried the crepes, she merely sprinkled them with granular white sugar and squeezed fresh lemon juice on top of them. She then rolled the crepes up like a loose cigar and put another sprinkle of sugar, then a splash of lemon juice, and a small dollop of whipped cream. They were out of this world. She said normally she used powdered sugar, but didn't have any at that moment. I don't think they could have been any better.

I've made crepes many times since then, and have found their potential unlimited. I use them for dessert, as mentioned above, or with ice cream wrapped inside, and chocolate fudge sauce all over. I use them wrapped around leftover meats and covered with cream soup, for a new entree. I wrap them around broiled seafood, and drizzle garlic and lemon butter over the top. Their possibilities are limited only by your imagination.

Ingredients	All-Dry
1½ teaspoons butter	2 teaspoons powder
1½ cups enriched flour	1½ cups
¼ teaspoon salt	¼ teaspoon
4 raw whole eggs, extra-large	8 tablespoons powder
2 cups whole milk	⅔ cup powder
¼ cup olive oil	4 mayonnaise portion packs
nil water	3 cups

Instructions: Combine butter, salt, and flour. Make a well in the flour mixture and put in the egg and milk. With a fork, whip the egg and milk together and gradually take up more and more flour until all is blended. Use a small amount of olive oil at a time to oil your skillet. Put one-eighth of a cup of batter into a hot, oiled skillet. Lift skillet from heat and rotate it until the batter is evenly spread over the bottom. Set skillet back on heat for one minute until batter is done. Separate the crepe from the skillet carefully to avoid tearing. Follow the same directions until all batter is made up into crepes. Serve as desired.

Note: If using all-dry ingredients, use the mayonnaise from single-portion packs to grease the skillet. It will not give the crepes a mayonnaise flavor. If convenient, you can still use olive oil instead of the mayonnaise.

Recipe Totals: 1,844 calories, 170 g carbohydrates (6 g dietary fiber and 29 g sugars), 1,070 mg cholesterol, 101 g total fat (28 g saturated fat), 64 g protein, 1,124 mg sodium.

Dietary Exchanges (recipe totals): Bread, 8.44; Fat, 16.9; Fruit, 0; Lean Meat, 4.42; Milk, 2; Vegetables, 0.

Remember to divide totals by the number of servings.

Fried Cakes

Servings: Makes about 20 cakes. Serves six to eight.

This recipe is an Historical Pioneer Trail Recipe from the *Cowboy Cookbook,* published by the Society for Range Management, which was kind enough to give me permission to reproduce a number of its historic recipes here. For these recipes I am listing the directions and recipes exactly as given. Occasionally, as in the case of beef fat, you will probably have to cook the fat down if you want to be authentic in your method of preparation.

Ingredients	All-Dry
1½ cups enriched flour	1½ cups
1 cup water	1¼ cups
½ cup beef fat drippings	⅓ cup shortening powder
1 teaspoon salt	1 teaspoon

Instructions: Combine flour with water. Mix well with a fork. Using plenty of flour on your hands and on a breadboard, roll out dough to a thickness of one quarter-inch. Cut into two-inch squares. Render beef fat in a skillet and add the squares of dough. Brown slowly on both sides. Sprinkle with salt to taste. Makes about 20 cakes.

(RECIPE COURTESY OF THE SOCIETY FOR RANGE MANAGEMENT)

Recipe Totals: 1,594 calories, 144 g carbohydrates (6 g dietary fiber and 3 g sugars), 112 mg cholesterol, 104 g total fat (52 g saturated fat), 19 g protein, 2,132 mg sodium.

Dietary Exchanges (recipe totals): Bread, 8.44; Fat, 24; Fruit, 0; Lean Meat, 0; Milk, 0; Vegetables, 0.

Remember to divide totals by the number of servings.

The Anatomy of the Chuck Wagon

❖ ❖ ❖

The mother ship for trail drives was a broad-beamed, sturdily built vehicle that carried virtually everything ten men might need on a prairie voyage lasting as long as five months. Credit for the ultimate design of the wagon belongs to cattle baron Charles Goodnight, who in 1866 rebuilt for his trail crew a surplus Army wagon, picked primarily for its extra-durable iron axles. To the basic wagon bed, where bulk goods such as foodstuffs and bedrolls were to be stored, Goodnight added three already customary traildrive appendages: on one side a water barrel big enough to hold two days' supply of water; on the other a heavy tool box; and on top bentwood bows to accommodate canvas covering for protection against sun and rain.

But the innovation that made the Goodnight wagon unique at the time, and a useful prototype for all self-respecting wagons that followed, was the design and installation of a chuck box. Perched at the rear of the wagon, facing aft, it had a hinged lid that led down onto a swinging leg to form a work table (side view in illustration). Like a Victorian desk, the box was honeycombed with drawers and cubbyholes (rear view in illustration). Here—and in the boot beneath—the cook stored his utensils and whatever food he might need during the day. A typical arrangement is shown in the illustration, with the most convenient of the niches occupied by the coffeepot and the whiskey bottle, the latter being in the cook's sole charge as medicine (to which cooks were known to be especially partial). Above them is the so-called "possible drawer," a combination first-aid kit and catchall, containing everything from calomel to sewing needles.

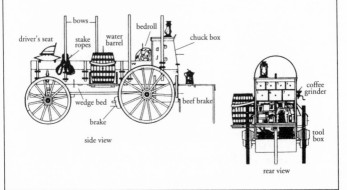

side view

rear view

The design of Goodnight's wagon proved so practical that cattle outfits all over the West imitated it, using redesigned farm wagons and Army vehicles. Inevitably the idea went commercial and become a standard item produced by major wagon builders, including the famous Studebaker Company, which sold chuck wagons for $75 to $100.

(From the *Trail Boss's Cowboy Cookbook*, courtesy of the Society for Range Management)

Fresh Apple Biscuits

Servings: Makes twelve. Serves six.

I like Chex cereal in these biscuits. It adds a nice texture to the bread as well as adding fiber and nutrients. I also like to use Total cereal for the added vitamin content.

Ingredients	All-Dry
1 cup Chex wheat cereal	1 cup
4 ounces raw apple, cored and grated	⅓ cup powder
½ cup canned or bottled apple juice	nil
2 cups Bisquik mix	2 cups
⅛ teaspoon ground allspice	⅛ teaspoon
1 teaspoon pure vanilla extract	¼ teaspoon powder
1 raw whole egg, extra-large	2 tablespoons powder
nil water	1¾ cups

Instructions: Mix all dry ingredients together, then add egg, apple, and juice. Drop by the spoonful on a greased baking sheet and bake for ten minutes at 450 degrees F.

Note: For those using all-dry ingredients, extra apple powder has been included to make up for omitting the apple juice.

Recipe Totals: 1,782 calories, 276 g carbohydrates (7 g dietary fiber and 31 g sugars), 247 mg cholesterol, 59 g total fat (16 g saturated fat), 39 g protein, 4,646 mg sodium.

Dietary Exchanges (recipe totals): Bread, 2; Fat, 0.581; Fruit, 2.24; Lean Meat, 1.1; Milk, 0; Vegetables, 0.

Remember to divide totals by the number of servings.

Flour Tortillas

Servings: Makes forty tortillas. Serves twenty.

I have listed this recipe exactly as it is given in the *Cowboy Cookbook*, published by the Society for Range Management (SRM). It was contributed to SRM by Dalton F. Merz, of Sonora, Texas, who got it from the man who cooks for his goat and sheep shearers.

This recipe is made for every meal for the 20-man shearing crew in the Sonora area. The tortillas are about one foot in diameter and vary in thickness from one-eighth inch to one-quarter inch. They are fried over an open fire of wood kindling on a piece of sheet metal about five feet square. Beans, eggs, or meat are usually rolled inside the tortillas. The unidentified cook is of Mexican origin and has about forty years of experience.

This is a great recipe and can be made anywhere. I realize that it makes an extremely large batch, but you can cut it down to any size you want.

Ingredients	All-Dry
10 cups enriched flour	10 cups
5 tablespoons double-acting baking powder	5 tablespoons
1 tablespoon salt	1 tablespoon
3 cups water	3 cups

Instructions: Mix dry ingredients then add water and mix until tough. Let stand 30 minutes. Divide dough to make about 40 tortillas. Knead individual tortillas, using dry flour on your hands and the mixing board to avoid sticking. Roll with a rolling pin (an eighteen-inch long or so section of a broomstick makes a nice roller). Flip each tortilla over after every pass with the roller.

(RECIPE COURTESY OF THE SOCIETY FOR RANGE MANAGEMENT)

Recipe Totals: 4,499 calories, 982 g carbohydrates (41 g dietary fiber and 22 g sugars), 0 mg cholesterol, 13 g total fat (0 g saturated fat), 125 g protein, 13,720 mg sodium.

Dietary Exchanges (recipe totals): Bread, 56.2; Fat, 0; Fruit, 0; Lean Meat, 0; Milk, 0; Vegetables, 0.

Remember to divide totals by the number of servings.

Homemade Corn Biscuits

Servings: Makes six to eight biscuits

When you want cornbread, but prefer the convenience of a biscuit, make these cornmeal biscuits. They are great with soups and stews. This mix can also be dropped by the spoonful into boiling stew for cornmeal dumplings; in that case, however, I recommend you make only half the recipe and leave out the butter and sugar.

Ingredients	All-Dry
½ cup self-rising enriched white cornmeal	½ cup
1½ cups enriched flour	1½ cups
1 teaspoon double-acting baking powder	1 teaspoon
½ teaspoon baking soda	½ teaspoon
⅓ cup butter oil (ghee)	⅓ cup butter powder
1 cup cultured buttermilk	⅓ cup powder
¼ cup white granulated sugar	¼ cup
nil water	1¾ cups

Instructions: Combine melted butter or butter oil with buttermilk. Add dry ingredients and mix well. Drop spoonfuls into a bowl or bag of flour and pat into biscuits. Bake for twenty minutes at 400 degrees F.

Note: When you're using all-dry ingredients, add water gradually to form a moist stiff dough only.

Recipe Totals: 1,760 calories, 250 g carbohydrates (10 g dietary fiber and 65 g sugars), 182 mg cholesterol, 73 g total fat (44 g saturated fat), 32 g protein, 2,138 mg sodium.

Dietary Exchanges (recipe totals): Bread, 8.44; Fat, 10.5; Fruit, 3.25; Lean Meat, 0; Milk, 1.1; Vegetables, 0.

Remember to divide totals by the number of servings.

Italian Garlic Muffins

Servings: Makes twenty muffins. Serves eight to ten.

These muffins are great any time, but they are especially good with pasta. Make more than you think you'll need—they have a tendency to disappear quickly.

Ingredients	All-Dry
¼ cup unsalted margarine	⅛ cup shortening powder
½ teaspoon garlic powder	½ teaspoon
2 teaspoons Italian seasoning	2 teaspoons
4½ cups biscuit mix	4½ cups
1 cup shredded whole-milk mozzarella cheese	⅔ cup freeze-dried
1¼ cups 2 percent low-fat milk with vitamin A	½ cup powder
nil water	1⅓ cups

Instructions: Combine margarine, flour, garlic, and Italian seasoning.Gradually add milk then fold in cheese. Bake at 375 degrees F for fifteen to twenty minutes.

Recipe Totals: 1,412 calories, 98 g carbohydrates (0.5 g dietary fiber and 18 g sugars), 111 mg cholesterol, 95 g total fat (32 saturated fat), 43 g protein, 2,173 mg sodium.
Dietary Exchanges (recipe totals): Bread, 0; Fat, 13.7; Fruit, 0; Lean Meat, 3.13; Milk, 1.25; Vegetables, 0.167.
Remember to divide totals by the number of servings.

Mile-High Biscuits

Servings: Makes twelve large biscuits. Serves six to eight.

Biscuit" seems such a common name for such an uncommonly wonderful bread. These biscuits are different from most because they contain egg. They're a cross between a biscuit and a roll. My mom would have called these party biscuits. This recipe calls for cream of tartar (tartaric acid), which helps the biscuits to rise higher, but you can accomplish the same thing by using buttermilk instead of the plain milk if you are out of cream of tartar.

Ingredients	All-Dry
3 cups enriched flour	3 cups
2 tablespoons white granulated sugar	⅛ cup
1½ tablespoons double-acting baking powder	1½ tablespoons
¾ teaspoon cream of tartar	¾ teaspoon
¾ teaspoon salt	¾ teaspoon
¾ cup butter oil (ghee)	¾ cup shortening powder
1 raw whole egg, extra-large	2 tablespoons powder
1 cup whole milk	⅓ cup powder
nil water	2 cups

Instructions: Combine dry ingredients. Work egg and butter oil in. Add milk and work into a dough ball. Knead dough until well blended. Roll out and cut biscuits one inch thick, or drop spoonfuls into flour and pat into biscuits. Bake for fifteen to twenty minutes at 450 degrees F.

Note: If you're using all-dry ingredients, add water gradually until the mixture forms a moist but stiff ball of dough. Not all flours require the same amount of water and you may need more or less. I used White Lily Flour to make these. It was the only flour my mother would use.

Recipe Totals: 1,400 calories, 284 g carbohydrates (20 g dietary fiber and 44 g sugars), 17 mg cholesterol, 14 g total fat (4 g saturated fat), 42 g protein, 3,994 mg sodium.

Dietary Exchanges (recipe totals): Bread, 16.9; Fat, 26.1; Fruit, 1.63; Lean Meat, 1.1; Milk, 1; Vegetables, 0.

Remember to divide totals by the number of servings.

Outback Damper Bread

Servings: Makes ten to twelve servings.

This recipe is from the *Cowboy Cookbook* by the Society for Range Management. It was given to them by June Southwood, of Australia. It was made popular by the fact that when bread was not obtainable the cook could make damper in a relatively short while. It's an easy-to-make recipe, generally enjoyed by those camping, and becoming increasingly popular at backyard barbecues.

This recipe calls for a camp oven (Dutch oven) which Ms. Southwood says is a cast-iron saucepan on three legs. It has a fitted lid and is one of the most-used cooking utensils in the outback of Australia. (The cottage loaf she recommends is a round loaf with a second, smaller, loaf pressed into its top. Elizabeth

David, in her book, *English Bread and Yeast Cookery*, described it as a loaf of bread with a bonnet.)

Note: After baking this bread myself, I can see how it got its name. In the closed Dutch oven, the moisture collects on the lid of the pot and drips back down onto the bread while it is cooking, making the top of the bread damp. It was delicious, making me marvel that so few ingredients could taste so good.

Ingredients	All-Dry
6 cups enriched self-rising flour	6 cups
1 tablespoon double-acting baking powder	1 tablespoon
1 teaspoon salt	1 teaspoon
3 cups whole milk	1 cup powder
nil water	3 cups

Instructions: Mix flour, baking powder, salt, and warm milk into a spongy dough. Shape as for a cottage loaf. Place the camp oven on the fire and heat well before placing bread mix in it. Place the bread mixture in the camp oven and bake for thirty minutes. Serve with honey, butter, golden syrup, jam, etc., while still warm.

(RECIPE COURTESY OF THE SOCIETY FOR RANGE MANAGEMENT)

Recipe Totals: 3,007 calories, 586 g carbohydrates (20 g dietary fiber and 47 g sugars), 99 mg cholesterol, 32 g total fat (15 g saturated fat), 92 g protein, 14,010 mg sodium.
Dietary Exchanges (recipe totals): Bread, 31.9; Fat, 4.5; Fruit, 0; Lean Meat, 0; Milk, 3; Vegetables, 0.
Remember to divide totals by the number of servings.

Pierogis

Servings: Makes twelve to sixteen. Serves four.

Our cousins in Pennsylvania, Dick, Gayle, Tara, and Pam Padfield, first introduced me to pierogis. In fact, this is a variation of the first pierogi recipe that Gayle gave me. Gayle and I love to swap recipes and cookbooks. They visit us each summer and it is one of the high points of our summer. You wouldn't believe four people could laugh so much, or have so much fun. They are not only family, they are our dear friends.

The recipe is of Polish origin, but there are Russian piroshes also. It is a nice change from regular pasta, and it is a very filling entree. My cousins use lots of different fillings for pierogis and piroshes: cabbage, mushrooms, and sauerkraut, as well as meats and fruits. Because it is a boiled dumpling, it can conveniently be made almost anywhere you can boil water.

Ingredients	All-Dry
2 cups enriched flour	2 cups
1 teaspoon salt	1 teaspoon
1 teaspoon butter	1 teaspoon shortening powder
3 raw whole eggs, extra-large	6 tablespoons powder
1 large fresh or frozen egg white	2 tablespoons powder
3 tablespoons distilled water	3 cups
1 cup mashed potatoes with whole milk	½ cup dried
½ cup shredded Cheddar cheese	⅓ cup freeze-dried
1 raw whole egg, extra-large	3 tablespoons powder
½ teaspoon salt	½ teaspoon
¼ teaspoon white pepper	¼ teaspoon
⅛ ounce mustard powder	⅛ teaspoon
½ cup butter	½ cup powder
¼ cup chopped fresh parsley	⅛ cup

Instructions:

(1) **Pierogi:** In a bowl, combine flour, one teaspoon salt, one tea-spoon butter, three tablespoons water, and three eggs. Work into a stiff dough. Turn dough out onto a floured surface and knead until smooth. Roll until less than one-eighth inch thick. Cut into three-inch disks.

(2) **Filling:** In a bowl, combine potatoes, shredded cheese, one whole egg, egg white, salt, pepper, mustard powder, and a quarter-cup butter. Blend. Spoon one tablespoon of mixture in the middle of the pierogi dough. Fold dough in half and seal edges with the tines of a fork.

(3) **Cooking:** Bring two to three quarts of water to a boil. Drop pierogis into the boiling water. Do not crowd them. Cook about eight to ten minutes or until they float. Remove and drain. Continue until all are cooked. Pour the remaining quarter-cup of butter and parsley over all, and serve warm.

Recipe Totals: 2,520 calories, 236 g carbohydrates (13 g dietary fiber and 11 g sugars), 1,311 mg cholesterol, 143 g total fat (80 g saturated fat), 78 g protein, 5,519 mg sodium.

Dietary Exchanges (recipe totals): Bread, 13.3; Fat, 23.9; Fruit, 0; Lean Meat, 6.73; Milk, 0; Vegetables, 0.217.

Remember to divide totals by the number of servings.

Mormon Johnnycake

Servings: Makes sixteen squares. Serves eight to ten.

This recipe is a Historical Pioneer Trail Recipe from the *Cowboy Cookbook*, published by the Society for Range Management. It is given exactly as listed. Enjoy!

Ingredients	All-Dry
2 cups whole-grain yellow cornmeal	2 cups
½ cup enriched flour	½ cup
1 teaspoon baking soda	1 teaspoon
1 teaspoon salt	1 teaspoon
2 cups cultured buttermilk	⅔ cup powder
2 tablespoons blackstrap cane molasses	1 tablespoon molasses powder
nil water	2⅛ cups

Instructions: Combine cornmeal, flour, baking soda, and salt. Stir in buttermilk and molasses. Pour batter into a greased nine-inch pan and bake in a 425-degree F oven for about twenty minutes. Cut into sixteen squares.

Note: To make a lighter cake, add two beaten eggs and two tablespoons melted butter to buttermilk, and cook about twenty-five minutes.

(RECIPE COURTESY OF THE SOCIETY FOR RANGE MANAGEMENT)

Recipe Totals: 1,400 calories, 284 g carbohydrates (20 g dietary fiber and 42 g sugars), 17 mg cholesterol, 14 g total fat (4 g saturated fat), 42 g protein, 4,015 mg sodium.

Dietary Exchanges (recipe totals): Bread, 12.8; Fat, 0; Fruit, 1.54; Lean Meat, 0; Milk, 2.21; Vegetables, 0.

Remember to divide totals by the number of servings.

Short-Cut Biscuits

Servings: Makes eight to ten. Serves four.

Despite their name, these "biscuits" are really more like crusty dinner rolls. They are very easy to fix, and no one will believe you at first when you tell them how you made them. My doctor, David Farley, says he makes them with fat-free mayonnaise, with good results.

Ingredients

	All-Dry
2 cups enriched flour	2 cups
½ cup mayonnaise	8 portion packs
½ cup whole milk	⅙ cup powder
1 teaspoon double-acting baking powder	1 teaspoon
nil water	¾ cup

Instructions: Combine dry ingredients with mayonnaise, and gradually add milk, making a soft dough. Roll and cut into biscuits or drop by the spoonful into extra flour then remove and pat out biscuit shape. Bake at 400 degrees F for twenty minutes or until lightly browned.

Recipe Totals: 1,761 calories, 203 g carbohydrates (8 g dietary fiber and 12 g sugars), 82 mg cholesterol, 94 g total fat (16 g saturated fat), 30 g protein, 1,175 mg sodium.
Dietary Exchanges (recipe totals): Bread, 11.3; Fat, 16.8; Fruit, 0; Lean Meat, 0; Milk, 0.5; Vegetables, 0.
Remember to divide totals by the number of servings.

Pan De Elate (Hot Pepper-Cheese Bread)

Servings: Makes six to eight servings.

This is a bread and a sandwich all in one. It is wonderful with chili or tomato soup. In fact, it's a meal in itself.

Ingredients

	All-Dry
2 cups canned creamed corn	1½ cups freeze-dried
6 ounces biscuit mix	1 cup
1 raw whole egg, extra-large	2 tablespoons powder
2 tablespoons butter oil (ghee)	2 tablespoons shortening powder
2 tablespoons white granulated sugar	2 tablespoons
½ cup whole milk	⅙ cup powder
½ cup canned hot green chili peppers, not drained	⅛ cup jalapeños, diced, dehydrated
1⅔ cup shredded Monterey Jack cheese	1⅓ cups freeze-dried
nil water	2¼ cups

Instructions: Mix all ingredients except chilies and cheese. Pour half of batter into a greased pan and top with chilies, then cheese. Pour remaining batter over all. Bake at 400 degrees F for thirty-five to forty minutes.

Note: When using all-dry ingredients, put the jalapeños in half a cup of water for about five minutes to rehydrate. Then follow the recipe as above, but drain the peppers before placing them on the batter.

Recipe Totals: 2,890 calories, 227 g carbohydrates (8 g dietary fiber and 53 g sugars), 652 mg cholesterol, 173 g total fat (97 g saturated fat), 123 g protein, 6,831 mg sodium.
Dietary Exchanges (recipe totals): Bread, 3.54; Fat, 19.8; Fruit, 1.63; Lean Meat, 13.9; Milk, 0.5; Vegetables, 1.67.
Remember to divide totals by the number of servings.

Parmesan Poppy-Seed Rolls

Servings: Makes sixteen rolls. Serves eight.

I used to associate poppy seeds with sweet rolls, or as a decoration for the tops of egg rolls. That was before I discovered how much nutritional value they could add to other breads. Now, I use them quite often. This recipe is a good example.

Ingredients	All-Dry
3 cups biscuit mix	3 cups
¾ cup cultured buttermilk	¼ cup powder
2 tablespoons dry Italian dressing mix	2 tablespoons
½ cup grated Parmesan cheese	½ cup
2 tablespoons butter oil (ghee)	2 tablespoons shortening powder
⅛ cup poppy seeds	⅛ cup
½ ounce grated Parmesan cheese	⅛ cup (reserve)
nil water	1 cup

Instructions: Combine biscuit mix, dry dressing mix, the half-cup of Parmesan, and poppy seeds. Add butter oil and gradually mix in buttermilk. Knead until smooth. Shape as desired and dip tops of rolls in the remaining Parmesan cheese. Bake at 375 to 400 degrees F for twenty minutes.

Recipe Totals: 2,404 calories, 294 g carbohydrates (2 g dietary fiber and 10 sugars), 97 mg cholesterol, 111 g total fat (41 g saturated fat), 60 g protein, 6,997 g sodium.
Dietary Exchanges (recipe totals): Bread, 0; Fat, 4.93; Fruit, 0; Lean Meat, 1.85; Milk, 0.827; Vegetables, 0.
Remember to divide totals by the number of servings.

Spicy Jalapeño Cornbread

Servings: Makes six servings.

This is more of a spoon bread than regular corn bread. If you like it hot and spicy, this is the one for you. My family loves this bread and sometimes when I don't have enough chili left over for another meal, I pour this bread in a hot greased skillet and put two cups of chili over the batter and top it with cheddar cheese. It all bakes up together in about thirty-five to forty minutes. You can serve it with salsa and sour cream if you really like Mexican food (and calories)! It's a great dollar-stretcher.

Ingredients	All-Dry
1 cup enriched flour	1 cup
¾ cup self-rising, enriched white cornmeal	¾ cup
¼ cup white granulated sugar	¼ cup
1 tablespoon double-acting baking powder	1 tablespoon
1 teaspoon salt	1 teaspoon
1 raw whole egg, extra-large	2 tablespoons powder
6 ounces canned yellow corn, not drained	1 cup freeze-dried
1 ounce canned chopped jalapeño peppers	1 tablespoon dehydrated
¼ cup olive oil	¼ cup shortening powder
1 tablespoon olive oil	1-portion pack mayonnaise
1¼ cups whole milk	½ cup milk powder
nil water	2¾ cups

Instructions: Combine flour, cornmeal, sugar, baking powder and salt. Add corn, liquid and all, and egg. Blend well. Add peppers and the quarter-cup of olive oil. Have skillet or baking pan hot, with one tablespoon olive oil in it. Pour batter into hot oiled pan. Remove immediately to the oven to bake.

Recipe Totals: 1,934 calories, 256 g carbohydrates (12 g dietary fiber and 71 g sugars), 289 mg cholesterol, 89 g total fat (18 g saturated fat), 41 g protein, 5,806 mg sodium.

Dietary Exchanges (recipe totals): Bread, 6.95; Fat, 15.6; Fruit, 3.25; Lean Meat, 1.1; Milk, 1.25; Vegetables, 0.417.

Remember to divide totals by the number of servings.

Pepper Cheese Biscuits

Servings: Makes twenty-four biscuits. Serves twelve.

These are great for snacking on during the day when you need a little some-thing to keep you going. They can also be made very thin, and fried crisp like a cracker. They will really give a new twist to peanut butter and crackers.

Ingredients	All-Dry
2 cups shredded Cheddar cheese	1½ cups freeze-dried
½ cup olive oil	½ cup shortening powder
1 tablespoon Worcestershire sauce	½ tablespoon powder
2 cups enriched flour	2 cups
½ teaspoon salt	½ teaspoon
½ teaspoon red Cayenne pepper	½ teaspoon
1 cup chopped dried pecans	1 cup
nil water	¾ cup

Instructions: Combine all the dry ingredients, then add olive oil and Worcestershire sauce. Divide into twenty-four pieces and roll into balls. Place on greased baking sheet and flatten into biscuits. Bake at 350 degrees F for twenty minutes or until lightly browned.

Recipe Totals: 3,566 calories, 220 g carbohydrates (14 g dietary fiber and 12 g sugars), 237 mg cholesterol, 266 g total fat (69 g saturated fat), 91 g protein, 2,637 mg sodium.
Dietary Exchanges (recipe totals): Bread, 11.3; Fat, 46; Fruit, 1.57; Lean Meat, 9.01; Milk, 0; Vegetables, 0.
Remember to divide totals by the number of servings.

Will's Red Bread

Servings: Makes four to six biscuits

This quick recipe with many options was sent to me by one of my longtime customers and friends, Will O'Daix. He said my *BakePacker's Companion* had encouraged him to do a little experimenting on his own. It became Red Bread because he used strawberry Jell-O, but any flavor of gelatin will work just fine.

Will says that he adds water to the leftover Jell-O to make a beverage that he says tastes like powdered drinks on the market.

I think Will's bread recipe is terrific, and one that you will use often.

Ingredients	All-Dry
1 cup Bisquik	1 cup
1 teaspoon baking powder	1 teaspoon
1 ounce Jell-O	⅓ envelope
⅓ cup water	⅓ cup

Instructions: Combine Bisquik, baking powder, and Jell-O. Blend, then add water to form a soft dough. Drop by the spoonful in extra flour (if any), pat into biscuit or drip as is on greased pan. Bake ten to fifteen minutes at 350 degree F.

Recipe Totals: 718 calories, 109 g carbohydrates (0 g dietary fiber and 4 g sugars), 0 mg cholesterol, 26 g total fat (7 g saturated fat), 14 g protein, 2,630 mg sodium.
Dietary Exchanges (recipe totals): Bread, 0; Fat, NA; Fruit, .276; Lean Meat, 0; Milk, NA; Vegetables, NA.
Remember to divide totals by the number of servings.

Sesame Seed Twist

Servings: Makes twenty-four. Serves six.

Sesame seeds are sometimes referred to as "benne seeds." They have a mild, nutty flavor when toasted. If you want a nutritious bread that's quick to make, this is it.

Ingredients	All-Dry
1 cup enriched flour	1 cup
1½ teaspoons double-acting baking powder	1½ teaspoons
¼ teaspoon salt	¼ teaspoon
⅓ cup whole milk	⅛ cup powder
2 tablespoons whole, dried sesame seeds	2 tablespoons
¼ cup butter oil (ghee)	¼ cup shortening powder
nil water	¾ cup

Instructions: Combine all the dry ingredients including seeds. Add butter and milk. Turn out on a floured surface and knead. Roll into a twelve-inch by six-inch rectangle. Cut into twenty-four strips. Brush with extra butter and sprinkle extra seeds on top if desired. Twist the strips as you lay them on the baking sheet. Bake at 375 degrees F for fifteen or twenty minutes.

(see next page for recipe nutritional data)

Recipe Totals: 1,051 calories, 106 g carbohydrates (6 g dietary fiber and 6 g sugar), 142 mg cholesterol, 64 g total fat (35 g saturated fat), 19 g protein, 1,308 mg sodium.
Dietary Exchanges (recipe totals): Bread, 5.63; Fat, 10.5; Fruit, 0; Lean Meat, 0; Milk, 0.33; Vegetables, 0.
Remember to divide totals by the number of servings.

Whole-Wheat Flat Bread

Servings: Makes eight to twelve. Serves six.

Flat bread is easy to make and quick to cook, so it's ideal for boat and trail. You can vary this recipe infinitely by changing the flour you use, and by adding spices, seeds, and nuts.

Ingredients	All-Dry
⅛ cup white granulated sugar	⅛ cup
⅛ cup olive oil	⅛ cup shortening powder
¾ cup whole-wheat flour	¾ cup
¾ cup enriched flour	¾ cup
½ teaspoon double-acting baking powder	½ teaspoon
½ teaspoon baking soda	½ teaspoon
¼ teaspoon salt	¼ teaspoon
1 cup cultured buttermilk	⅓ cup powder
nil water	1 cup, plus 1 tablespoon

Instructions: In a bowl, combine sugar, oil, and buttermilk; then add salt, soda, and baking powder. Gradually mix in flours. Roll thin between two pieces of waxed paper or plastic wrap. Cut in squares. Bake at 375 degrees F for twelve minutes.

Recipe Totals: 1,076 calories, 175 g carbohydrates (14 g dietary fiber and 40 g sugars), 9 mg cholesterol, 32 g total fat (5 g saturated fat), 30 g protein, 1,137 mg sodium.
Dietary Exchanges (recipe totals): Bread, 7.97; Fat, 5.24; Fruit, 1.63; Lean Meat, 0; Milk, 1.1; Vegetables, 0.
Remember to divide totals by the number of servings.

* CHAPTER 5 *

Quick Sweet Breads

—🌾—

Muffins, scones, sweet breads, and tea cakes are a few of my favorite things. They are all varieties of quick breads and use baking powder or baking soda, plus an acidic ingredient, as leavening. As with non-sweet quick breads, all these items are ideal to bake on the trail or in a boat. As their grouping with the quick breads implies, they are quick to mix and bake, although some items are easier to bake than others.

Easy Fruit Loaf

Servings: Makes nine three-inch squares. Serves nine.

This recipe is very easy to make. I like to use pistachio pudding and frozen whipped cream mixed together for the frosting, and sometimes I add an extra pack of pistachio pudding to the cake batter.

Ingredients	All-Dry
7 ounces yellow cake mix	2 cups
¼ cup enriched, all-purpose white flour	¼ cup
1 raw whole egg, extra-large	2 tablespoons powder
1 cup fruit cocktail, undrained	1 cup freeze-dried
nil water	1¼ cups

Instructions: Combine all ingredients and pour in a greased and floured pan. Bake for forty to fifty minutes at 350 degrees F.

Note: If you're using freeze-dried fruit, add the water to the fruit and let it stand for three to five minutes. If you're using dehydrated fruit, reduce the amount of fruit to half a cup, cover it with boiling water, and let it stand for ten to fifteen minutes.

Recipe Totals: 1,150 calories, 201 g carbohydrates (4 g dietary fiber and 28 g sugars), 299 mg cholesterol, 30 g total fat (10 g saturated fat), 24 g protein, 1,608 mg sodium.

Dietary Exchanges (recipe totals): Bread, 5.38; Fat, 5.54; Fruit, 6.96; Lean Meat, 1.1; Milk, 0; Vegetables, 0.

Remember to divide totals by the number of servings.

Apple-Walnut Whiskey Bread

Servings: Makes one loaf. Serves four.

This is a moist bread with a wonderful flavor.

Ingredients	All-Dry
½ cup enriched flour	½ cup
¼ cup whole-wheat flour	¼ cup
¼ cup white granulated sugar	¼ cup
1 teaspoon double-acting baking powder	1 teaspoon
½ teaspoon baking soda	½ teaspoon
½ teaspoon salt	½ teaspoon
½ teaspoon cinnamon	½ teaspoon
¼ teaspoon ground allspice	¼ teaspoon
2 raw whole eggs, extra-large	4 tablespoons powder
¼ cup olive oil	¼ cup shortening powder
¼ cup apple butter	⅛ cup apple powder
½ cup chopped, dried English walnuts	½ cup
⅓ cup fresh, peeled apple slices	¼ cup dried
1 tablespoon whiskey (optional)	1 teaspoon wine powder
½ teaspoon pure vanilla extract	¼ teaspoon powder
3 cups water (for pressure cooker)	4¼ cups (1¼ for batter)

Instructions: Mix flours, sugar, baking powder, baking soda, salt, and spices. Stir in remaining ingredients except water. Pour into a greased loaf pan measuring six inches by two-and-a-quarter inches by two inches. Cover pan securely with greased aluminum foil. Place cooking rack and three cups of water in a four- to six-quart pressure cooker. Place loaf pan on rack. Cover securely. Do not place pressure regulator on vent pipe. Heat until steam gently flows through vent pipe. Cook for forty-five minutes. Remove loaf and let cool on a wire rack.

(RECIPE COURTESY OF NATIONAL PRESTO INDUSTRIES)

Recipe Totals: 1,751 calories, 174 g carbohydrates (11 g dietary fiber and 91 g sugars), 494 mg cholesterol, 104 g total fat (15 g saturated fat), 34 g protein, 2,340 mg sodium.

Dietary Exchanges (recipe totals): Bread, 4.66; Fat, 11.6; Fruit, 5.55; Lean Meat, 2.21; Milk, 0; Vegetables, 0.

Remember to divide totals by the number of servings.

Apricot Nut Bread

Servings: Makes one loaf. Serves six to eight.

Apricots are very high in potassium and make very good snacks when you're on the boat or the trail. This nut bread will last several days or longer if you make the dough into a long, crescent-shaped loaf about two inches thick. After you've baked it according to the instructions below, slice it diagonally into half-inch-thick slices and pop them back in the oven for another twenty minutes on medium-low heat. This will dry them out and give them a light golden appearance. In other words, it will turn them into biscotti—a real treat.

Ingredients	All-Dry
2⅔ cups enriched flour	2⅔ cups
¾ cup white granulated sugar	¾ cup
3 teaspoons double-acting baking powder	3 teaspoons
½ teaspoon salt	½ teaspoon
2 raw whole eggs, extra-large	4 tablespoons powder
¼ cup olive oil	¼ cup shortening powder
1 cup cultured buttermilk	⅓ cup powder
1½ cups dried apricot halves	1½ cups diced
1 cup chopped, dried English walnuts	1 cup
nil water	1¾ cups

Instructions: Combine sugar and butter. Add egg. Add all other ingredients and blend well. Bake at 350 degrees F for forty-five to fifty-five minutes.

Recipe Totals: 3,762 calories, 566 g carbohydrates (32 g dietary fiber and 274 g sugars), 503 mg cholesterol, 146 g total fat (19 g saturated fat), 80 g protein, 2,968 mg sodium.
Dietary Exchanges (recipe totals): Bread, 16.2; Fat, 11.6; Fruit, 17.7; Lean Meat, 2.21; Milk, 1.1; Vegetables, 0.
Remember to divide totals by the number of servings.

Boston Plum Brown Bread

Servings: Makes two loaves. Serves twelve.

This bread is an old classic from Gretchen McMullen's "Testing Kitchen," at King Arthur Flour and contains very little fat. It is incredibly rich and moist because the liquid in the batter is locked in during the steaming process. Its name harks back to the time when raisins were called plums (as in plum pudding).

Brown bread is traditionally eaten with baked beans, another of those clever combinations that create a complete protein out of foods that contain only incomplete proteins. With or without beans, this bread is a nutritious winner.

Ingredients	All-Dry
1 cup whole-grain yellow cornmeal	1 cup
1 cup medium rye flour	1 cup
1 cup multipurpose white wheat flour	1 cup
1 teaspoon baking soda	1 teaspoon
1 teaspoon salt	1 teaspoon
1 cup packed seedless raisins	1 cup
2 cups cultured buttermilk	⅔ cup powder
¾ cup blackstrap cane molasses	⅓ cup powder
nil water	2¾ cups

Instructions: Mix the cornmeal, flours, baking soda, salt, and raisins together. In a separate bowl, combine the buttermilk and molasses, and add them to the dry ingredients. Place the mixture in two, greased one-pound coffee cans or one two-quart pudding mold, filling them two-thirds full. Cover them loosely with foil that has been greased on the underside, and secure with a rubber band.

Place the cans in a kettle or saucepan on top of an inverted pie tin or cake pan or something to keep the cans off the bottom of the kettle. The kettle or saucepan should be deep enough for the lid to fit, covering the cans of bread mixture. Fill the kettle with boiling water two-thirds of the way up the cans. Cover, bring the water back to a boil, and lower the heat to a simmer. Steam your pudding for about two hours, adding water if necessary.

(RECIPE COURTESY OF KING ARTHUR FLOUR)

Recipe Totals: 2,446 calories, 560 g carbohydrates (43 g dietary fiber and 262 g sugars), 17 mg cholesterol, 13 g total fat (4 g saturated fat), 56 g protein, 4,112 mg.

Dietary Exchanges (recipe totals): Bread, 9.55; Fat, 0; Fruit, 17.2; Lean Meat, 0; Milk, 2.21; Vegetables, 0.

Remember to divide totals by the number of servings.

Cherry Tart Muffins

Servings: Makes sixteen. Serves eight to ten.

My cherry trees are in bloom outside and they are lovely. Once again, I wonder if the birds will leave me a few cherries to use in my cooking. I can't complain too much because I like to look at the birds—and the sweetened dried Montmorency tart cherries now available in the stores are wonderful. It's just like eating a cherry pie without the crust. They are what make this muffin special.

Ingredients	All-Dry
2½ cups enriched flour	2½ cups
1 tablespoon double-acting baking powder	1 tablespoon
1 cup white granulated sugar	1 cup
¼ teaspoon salt	¼ teaspoon
1 cup cultured buttermilk	⅓ cup powder
2 raw whole eggs, extra-large	4 tablespoons powder
¼ cup butter oil (ghee)	¼ cup shortening powder
4 ounces dried Montmorency tart cherries with sugar	½ cup chopped
nil water	1¾ cups

Instructions: Reserve one-eighth cup sugar for tops. Combine remaining sugar, butter, and eggs. Blend well. Add all other ingredients and blend. Put in muffin cups and sprinkle tops with sugar. Bake at 400 degrees F for thirty minutes.

Recipe Totals: 3,004 calories, 551 g carbohydrates (13 g dietary fiber and 296 g sugars), 634 mg cholesterol, 68 g total fat (37 g saturated fat), 87 g protein, 2,407 mg sodium.

Dietary Exchanges (recipe totals): Bread, 14.1; Fat, 9.15; Fruit, 13; Lean Meat, 2.21; Milk, 1.1; Vegetables, 0.

Remember to divide totals by the number of servings.

Cranberry Streusel Muffins

Servings: Makes six to eight muffins. Serves four.

These muffins are delicious. They're perfect for a special breakfast or mid-morning snack. I like to use the cranberry sauce with whole cranberries in it, and now that some of the food companies offer flavored cranberry chutney, I've used that too. Both work well. The streusel topping really adds a nice touch, but on the trail or boat, granola sprinkled on top before baking works just as well.

Ingredients	All-Dry
1 tablespoon all-purpose enriched white flour	1 tablespoon
2 tablespoons packed brown sugar	2 tablespoons
½ teaspoon cinnamon	½ teaspoon
1 tablespoon unsalted butter	1 tablespoon shortening powder
2 cups canned cranberry sauce	1 cup dried
1½ cups prepared biscuit mix	1½ cups
3 tablespoons white granulated sugar	3 tablespoons
1 raw whole egg, extra-large	2 tablespoons powder
⅔ cup 2 percent, low-fat milk with vitamin A	¼ cup powder
nil water	2⅔ cups

Instructions: Combine first four ingredients (the streusel topping) and set aside. In another bowl, combine sugar and egg. Stir in milk, then biscuit mix. Dice cranberry sauce into half-inch cubes and fold into mix. Do not stir too long or the cubes will blend into the mix completely. Spoon into greased muffin tins or loaf tin. Sprinkle streusel topping over mix and bake at 375 degrees F for about 20 minutes until puffed.

Note: If you're using dry cranberries, let them to come to a boil in one cup of the water, then set them aside to cool, and mix as above. The remaining water is for the milk powder.

Recipe Totals: 2,407 calories, 421 g carbohydrates (12 g dietary fibers and 250 g sugars), 305 mg cholesterol, 65 g total fat (21 g saturated fat), 41 g protein, 3,757 mg sodium.

Dietary Exchanges (recipe totals): Bread, 11.2; Fat, 11.5; Fruit, 14.9; Lean Meat, 1.1; Milk, 0.67; Vegetables, 0.

Remember to divide totals by the number of servings.

Doughnut Muffins

Servings: Makes twelve doughnuts. Serves six.

These are just the thing with a cup of milk, coffee, or tea. You can vary the spices and flavorings for a variety of new doughnut muffins.

Ingredients	All-Dry
⅓ cup vegetable shortening	¼ cup shortening powder
1 cup white granulated sugar	1 cup
1 raw whole egg, extra-large	2 tablespoons powder
1½ cups enriched, all-purpose white flour	1½ cups
1½ teaspoons double-acting baking powder	1½ teaspoons
¼ teaspoon ground nutmeg	¼ teaspoon
½ teaspoon salt	½ teaspoon
½ cup 2 percent low-fat milk with vitamin A	⅙ cup powder
6 tablespoons unsalted butter	⅓ cup powder
1 teaspoon cinnamon	1 teaspoon
nil water	1½ cups

Instructions: Combine all ingredients except six tablespoons melted butter, one tablespoon sugar, and one teaspoon cinnamon. Bake in muffin cups for twenty to thirty minutes at 350 degrees F. When light brown, and muffin springs back to the touch, remove from oven and dip in melted butter, then roll top in cinnamon-sugar mixture.

Note: When using all-dry ingredients, mix the sugar, cinnamon, and butter powder for the topping; dip the hot muffin tops in the dry mix, then cover the muffins for a minute or two. The steam from the hot muffins will provide the moisture necessary for the topping.

Recipe Totals: 2,769 calories, 342 g carbohydrates (7 g dietary fiber and 210 g sugars), 442 mg cholesterol, 147 g total fat (62 g saturated fat), 30 g protein, 1,948 mg sodium.

Dietary Exchanges (recipe totals): Bread, 6.92; Fat, 19.1; Fruit, 13; Lean Meat, 1.1; Milk, 0.5; Vegetables, 0.

Remember to divide totals by the number of servings.

Date Nut Bread

Servings: Makes one loaf. Serves six to eight.

My mom served date nut bread and cream cheese sandwiches for special treats. This is a good bread to cook in the pressure cooker if you have one. I save green-bean cans that have an enamel lining (like Hanover Foods or Libby's), and bake in those, or use wide-mouth pint jars. If you're on a boat, you could make several in the pint jars and then heat-seal them with canning lids when they are done. That would give you a good snack or dessert item on those days when baking is far from your mind.

Ingredients	All-Dry
4 cups chopped dates	4 cups
4 cups chopped, dried English walnuts	4 cups
4 cups enriched flour	4 cups
1 teaspoon salt	1 teaspoon
1½ cups packed brown sugar	1½ cups
2 raw whole eggs, extra-large	4 tablespoons powder
2 teaspoons baking soda	2 teaspoons
2 cups, boiling water	2½ cups

Instructions: Pour two cups boiling water over dates, set aside. Combine sugar and eggs. If you're working with powdered eggs, add half a cup of water. Add all other ingredients to egg mixture, including dates, and any liquid left in dates. Bake in a greased loaf pan for fifty to fifty-five minutes at 350 degrees F.

Recipe Totals: 8,238 calories, 1,318 g carbohydrates (92 g dietary fiber and 811 g sugars), 484 mg cholesterol, 317 g total fat (32 g saturated fat), 147 g protein, 4,998 mg sodium.

Dietary Exchanges (recipe totals): Bread, 27.3; Fat, 1.16; Fruit, 52.5; Lean Meat, 2.21; Milk, 0; Vegetables, 0.

Remember to divide totals by the number of servings.

Edinburgh Lemon Loaf

Servings: Makes two loaves. Serves twelve.

My grandfather was born in Edinburgh, Scotland, and was a stone carver of some note both there and here in the United States. He was carrying on the family trade, as my great-grandfather was one of the carvers of the statue of Sir Walter Scott, on the square in Edinburgh.

This recipe has its origin in the Scottish Highlands. It's a wonderful tea bread with no fat added to the mix—the eggs take care of that. The original recipe called for regular raisins, but I like the combination of golden raisins and lemon.

Ingredients	All-Dry
4 cups enriched flour	4 cups
1 cup white granulated sugar	1 cup
1 tablespoon double-acting baking powder	1 tablespoon
1 tablespoon fresh lemon peel	½ tablespoon dry granules
2 raw whole eggs, extra-large	4 tablespoons powder
1 cup whole milk	⅓ cup powder
1 pound packed golden seedless raisins	1 pound
nil water	1½ cups plus 1 tablespoon

Instructions: Combine all the dry ingredients, raisins, and lemon peel. Make a well in the dry mixture and add eggs and one cup of milk. Using a fork, whip eggs and milk together and then gradually blend more and more of the flour until all is mixed. Place the dough in a greased and floured loaf pan and bake at 350 degrees F for thirty-five to forty minutes or until the loaf is slightly brown and springs back to the touch.

Recipe Totals: 4,261 calories, 963 g carbohydrates (33 g dietary fiber and 564 g sugars), 527 mg cholesterol, 27 g total fat (9 g saturated fat), 88 g protein, 1,788 mg sodium.

Dietary Exchanges (recipe totals): Bread, 22.5; Fat, 2.66; Fruit, 35; Lean Meat, 2.21; Milk, 1; Vegetables, 0.

Remember to divide totals by the number of servings.

English Digestive Biscuit

Servings: Makes forty-eight biscuits. Serves eight.

King Arthur Flour was kind enough to let me use this recipe. I was particularly interested in it because I love the English countryside murder mysteries whose characters are always eating "digestive biscuits." Now I know what they're eating.

The King Arthur Flour Company says, "Digestive biscuits are as English as Peter Pan. They're in the never-never-land between cookies and crackers, a perfect in-between sort of biscuit for an in-between sort of meal." Developed during the latter part of the nineteenth century to increase the fiber in Victorian diets, they are best described as a sophisticated graham cracker.

Ingredients	All-Dry
½ cup multipurpose white wheat flour	½ cup
1½ cups whole-wheat flour	1½ cups
1 teaspoon double-acting baking powder	1 teaspoon
½ cup butter	½ cup shortening powder
¾ cup sifted white powdered sugar	¾ cup powder
¼ cup whole milk	⅛ cup powder
nil water	¾ cup

Instructions: Combine dry ingredients in a bowl and mix in butter until crumbly. Add enough milk to make a stiff dough. Knead this mixture on a floured surface until smooth. Return to bowl and let rest for between ten and thirty minutes—chill it during this time if possible. Preheat oven to 350 degrees F. Roll dough out to a thickness of slightly more than one-eighth inch. Cut into biscuits: the traditional size is two-and-a-half inches in diameter. Using a fork, prick the tops of the biscuits evenly and bake for fifteen to twenty minutes on a greased cookie sheet until pale gold.

(RECIPE COURTESY OF KING ARTHUR FLOUR)

Recipe Totals: 1,941 calories, 251 g carbohydrates (27 g dietary fiber and 81 g sugars), 257 mg cholesterol, 98 g total fat (59 g saturated fat), 35 g protein, 1,468 mg sodium.
Dietary Exchanges (recipe totals): Bread, 7.51; Fat, 18.5; Fruit, 4.88; Lean Meat, 0; Milk, 0.25; Vegetables, 0.
Remember to divide totals by the number of servings.

Fresh Orange Tea Cakes

Servings: Makes twelve. Serves six.

When I was a child, my mom used to make tea cakes a lot. They aren't quite a cake, or a cookie, but something in between. I still fix tea cakes like my mom. When I'm not too busy, I roll them out about a half-inch thick and cut them with a three-inch-diameter biscuit cutter. Sugar sprinkled on generously before baking is good. Cream cheese frosting, added after baking, is another favorite of mine. I think that once you try these they will win your devotion too.

Ingredients	All-Dry
2 cups enriched flour	2 cups
¼ teaspoon cream of tartar	¼ teaspoon
1 cup unsalted butter	⅔ cup shortening powder
1¼ cups white granulated sugar	1¼ cups
2 raw whole eggs, extra-large	4 tablespoons powder
½ cup fresh orange juice	⅛ teaspoon powdered extract
1½ tablespoons grated fresh orange peel	½ tablespoon dried
¼ cup fresh lemon juice	1 tablespoon powder
2 teaspoons double-acting baking powder	2 teaspoons
nil water	1¼ cups

For Cream Cheese Frosting

1 cup powdered sugar	1 cup
¼ cup butter	¼ cup powdered
¼ cup cream cheese	¼ cup powdered
nil water	⅛ to ¼ cup

Instructions: Combine all the dry ingredients, then mix in butter until crumbly. Add peel, eggs, and juices. Mix well. Drop dinnerspoonfuls onto a greased cookie sheet and flatten with a fork. Sprinkle with additional sugar if desired. Bake at 375 degrees F for ten minutes or until light brown.

Note: If you're using all-dry ingredients, you can eliminate the orange juice powder entirely if unavailable, and add about an eighth teaspoon of citric acid to the dry ingredients for the slight tartness needed.

(see next page for recipe nutritional data)

Recipe Totals (sans frosting): 3,745 calories, 46 g carbohydrates (9 g dietary fiber and 273 g sugars), 991 mg cholesterol, 198 g total fat (118 g saturated fat), 43 g protein, 1,153 mg sodium.

Dietary Exchanges (recipe totals): Bread, 1.3; Fat, 49; Fruit, 17.6; Lean Meat, 2.21; Milk, 0; Vegetables, 0.

Remember to divide totals by the number of servings.

Honey-Wheat Blueberry Muffins

Servings: Makes twelve. Serves six.

These muffins are high in fiber and nutrition. If you add extra water or milk, you can also have some of the best whole-grain pancakes ever.

Ingredients	All-Dry
1 cup enriched flour	1 cup
1 cup whole-wheat flour	1 cup
½ cup toasted wheat germ	½ cup
½ cup honey	⅓ cup powder
1 raw whole egg, extra-large	2 tablespoons powder
⅓ cup olive oil	⅓ cup shortening powder
⅓ cup whole dry milk powder	⅓ cup
1 tablespoon double-acting baking powder	1 tablespoon
4 ounces wild blueberries	½ cup
1 cup water	2 cups

Instructions: Combine all dry ingredients, then add honey, oil, and warm water. Spoon into muffin tins and bake for twenty minutes at 375 degrees F.

Note: If making pancakes, increase the water to two cups for the regular mix, and for all-dry ingredients increase the water to three cups.

Recipe Totals: 2,912 calories, 465 g carbohydrates (39 g dietary fiber and 226 g sugars), 286 mg cholesterol, 100 g total fat (20 g saturated fat), 66 g protein, 1,720 mg sodium.

Dietary Exchanges (recipe totals): Bread, 12.6; Fat, 16.5; Fruit, 8; Lean Meat, 2.23; Milk, 1.28; Vegetables, 0.

Remember to divide totals by the number of servings.

Maple-Pecan Cornbread

Servings: Makes six to eight servings.

I know this recipe sounds strange, but it's wonderful. It's not too sweet to serve with a meal. I like to take the leftover cornbread, split it in half, and toast it with a little margarine in my skillet. I then serve it with maple syrup for breakfast. Having it for breakfast is a good enough reason to bake it for dinner.

Ingredients	All-Dry
1 cup enriched all-purpose white flour	1 cup
1 cup yellow cornmeal, self-rising	1 cup
1 teaspoon double-acting baking powder	1 teaspoon
1 teaspoon baking soda	1 teaspoon
1 teaspoon salt	1 teaspoon
3 tablespoons packed brown sugar	3 tablespoons
3 tablespoons unsalted margarine	2 tablespoons shortening powder
2 (each) raw whole eggs, extra-large	4 tablespoons powder
⅓ cup maple syrup	¼ cup powder
¾ cup cultured buttermilk	¼ cup powder
½ cup chopped dried pecans	½ cup
nil water	1⅔ cups

Instructions: Combine all ingredients. Pour into a hot buttered skillet or Dutch oven and bake at 375 degrees F for thirty-five minutes.

Note: Instead of using pecans and maple, I occasionally use one small can of pineapple and one-third cup walnuts. If you try this, reduce the buttermilk to one-third cup.

Recipe Totals: 2,245 calories, 315 g carbohydrates (15 g dietary fiber and 123 g sugars), 501 mg cholesterol, 93 g total fat (15 saturated fat), 46 g protein, 5,771 mg sodium.

Dietary Exchanges (recipe totals): Bread, 5.66; Fat, 15.1; Fruit, 7.22; Lean Meat, 2.76; Milk, 0.827; Vegetables, 0.

Remember to divide totals by the number of servings.

Mrs. Humphries' Scones

Servings: Makes ten to twelve scones. Serves six.

This is another great recipe given to the King Arthur Flour Company by Mrs. Humphries. She is an elderly Englishwoman who lives across the street from one of their employees' parents. Her scones are rich and delicious.

Ingredients	All-Dry
1 cup multipurpose white wheat flour	1 cup
½ cup white granulated sugar	½ cup
2 teaspoons double-acting baking powder	2 teaspoons
3 tablespoons butter	2 tablespoons shortening powder
½ cup packed seedless raisins	½ cup
1 raw whole egg, extra-large	2 tablespoons powder
⅛ ounce oil of lemon	½ teaspoon powder
2 cups whole milk	⅔ cup powder
¼ cup white granulated sugar (for top)	¼ cup
nil water	2¼ cups

Instructions: Combine the flour, sugar, and baking powder. Work in the butter until mix is crumbly. Add raisins, eggs, and lemon extract. Use just enough milk to mix it into a soft—but not sticky—dough. Drop big tablespoonfuls of dough onto a greased cookie sheet. Sprinkle tops with the quarter-cup of granular sugar. Bake for twelve to fifteen minutes, depending on the size you make them.

(RECIPE COURTESY OF KING ARTHUR FLOUR)

Recipe Totals: 1,659 calories, 305 g carbohydrates (16 g dietary fiber and 219 g sugars), 347 mg cholesterol, 48 g total fat (25 g saturated fat), 27 g protein, 1,441 mg sodium.

Dietary Exchanges (recipe totals): Bread, 0; Fat, 7.68; Fruit, 13.8; Lean Meat, 1.1; Milk, 0.2; Vegetables, 0.

Remember to divide totals by the number of servings.

Orange-Cranberry Bread

Servings: Makes two medium loaves. Serves twelve.

I don't know what it is about the combination of orange and cranberry that makes it so special, but it is one of my favorites. I think this will become one of your favorites too.

Ingredients	All-Dry
2 cups enriched flour	2 cups
1 cup white granulated sugar	1 cup
1½ teaspoons baking soda	1½ teaspoons
1 teaspoon salt	1 teaspoon
1 teaspoon double-acting baking powder	1 teaspoon
¼ cup butter oil (ghee)	¼ cup shortening powder
1 raw whole egg, extra-large	2 tablespoons powder
1 tablespoon grated fresh orange peel	½ tablespoon dried
¾ cup fresh orange juice	⅓ cup powder
1½ cups packed golden seedless raisins	1½ cups
1½ cups cranberries	1 cup dried
nil water	2¾ cups

Instructions: Combine sugar and butter. Add egg and beat well. Add remaining ingredients. Pour into two medium greased and floured loaf pans. Bake at 350 degrees F for one hour or until it springs back when touched in the middle.

Note: When using dried cranberries, pour one-and-a-half cups of boiling water over the cranberries and let them steep for ten minutes or until cool. Mix as directed.

Recipe Totals: 3,111 calories, 630 g carbohydrates (22 g dietary fiber and 423 g sugars), 378 mg cholesterol, 61 g total fat (34 g saturated fat), 43 g protein, 4,621 mg sodium.

Dietary Exchanges (recipe totals): Bread, 11.3; Fat, 8.57; Fruit, 28.1; Lean Meat, 1.1; Milk, 0; Vegetables, 0.

Remember to divide totals by the number of servings.

Peach Bread

Servings: Makes one loaf. Serves six.

I like this bread best with fresh peaches, preferably off my own trees, but that doesn't happen often. We usually have a late frost in the mountains of North Carolina that kills the blossoms; maybe that's what makes them so good when they do produce peaches. I grew my trees from seed (the pit) and they are easy to grow. I just took a stick and made a hole about one inch deep and put the seed in the ground. Try growing your own trees, but remember you need two for cross-pollination. Next time you have a peach that tastes especially good, plant that seed.

Ingredients	All-Dry
2 cups enriched flour	2 cups
½ cup white granulated sugar	½ cup
½ cup packed brown sugar	½ cup
⅛ teaspoon salt	⅛ teaspoon
1 teaspoon baking soda	1 teaspoon
2 cups peeled, sliced peaches	1 cup dried
1 raw whole egg, extra-large	2 tablespoons
1 tablespoon butter oil (ghee)	1 tablespoon shortening powder
nil water	2½ cups, boiling

Instructions: Combine sugars, egg, and butter. Beat well. Add remaining ingredients and let stand for fifteen minutes before baking. Bake at 350 degrees F for forty-five to fifty-five minutes.

Note: If you're using dried peaches, add two-and-a-half cups of boiling water to them and let them steep for fifteen minutes. Then mix as directed, using peaches and liquid.

Recipe Totals: 2,038 calories, 438 g carbohydrates (14 g dietary fiber and 242 g sugars), 280 mg cholesterol, 21 g total fat (10 g saturated fat), 35 g protein, 1,645 mg sodium.

Dietary Exchanges (recipe totals): Bread, 11.3; Fat, 2.58; Fruit, 21.2; Lean Meat, 1.1; Milk, 0; Vegetables, 0.

Remember to divide totals by the number of servings.

Pecan-Mincemeat Muffins

Servings: Makes twelve muffins. Serves six.

This recipe makes me think of the holidays. In the past that's about the only time I've used mincemeat. If you buy mincemeat at the grocery store it's fairly expensive. That may have had something to do with my not using it often.

Last year, my apple tree had a delicious bumper crop. After forcing everyone who happened by to take home a sack of apples, I still had what seemed like tons of apples. I can't stand to see food go to waste, so I made just about everything that could possibly be made using apples, including mincemeat—without the meat. It turned out especially well, and this recipe is a good example of how I used it.

Ingredients	All-Dry
2 cups enriched flour	2 cups
1 teaspoon salt	1 teaspoon
1 tablespoon double-acting baking powder	1 tablespoon
1 raw whole egg, extra-large	2 tablespoons powder
¾ cup whole milk	¼ cup powder
3 tablespoons olive oil	3 tablespoons shortening powder
6 ounces mincemeat	1 cup (no substitute)
½ cup chopped dried pecans	½ cup
nil water	1⅛ cups

Instructions: Combine all ingredients. Spoon into greased and floured muffin tins. Bake at 350 degrees F for twenty minutes.

Note: While there is no prepared dehydrated substitute for mincemeat, you could use a quarter-cup dried apples and a quarter-cup raisins along with a half-teaspoon each of cinnamon and cloves, and a half-cup of additional water.

Recipe Totals: 2,345 calories, 298 g carbohydrates (15 g dietary fiber and 75 g sugars), 272 mg cholesterol, 114 g total fat (19 g saturated fat), 47 g protein, 4,193 mg sodium.

Dietary Exchanges (recipe totals): Bread, 13; Fat, 19.7; Fruit, 4.43; Lean Meat, 1.66; Milk, 0.75; Vegetables, 0.

Remember to divide totals by the number of servings.

Raisin Bran Muffins

Servings: Makes ten to twelve muffins. Serves six.

I love bran muffins. When I was in college, I would go to Morrisons' Cafeteria for their bran muffins. I thought they were the best. This recipe is a fair comparison. I like to use Br'er Rabbit blackstrap molasses to make them because it gives such a dark color to the muffin and a distinctive taste, but Grandma's molasses or any other will work fine. Adventure Foods also carries a powdered molasses that works well.

Ingredients	All-Dry
2 cups raisin bran cereal	2 cups
¾ cup white granulated sugar	¾ cup
1¼ cups enriched flour	1¼ cups
1 teaspoon double-acting baking powder	1 teaspoon
½ teaspoon salt	½ teaspoon
¼ cup butter oil (ghee)	¼ cup shortening powder
1 raw whole egg, extra-large	2 tablespoons powder
1 cup cultured buttermilk	⅓ cup powder
⅛ cup blackstrap molasses	⅛ cup powder
nil water	1¾ cups

Instructions: Combine egg, sugar, and butter. Add buttermilk, molasses, and raisin bran cereal. Let stand five minutes to soak and soften. Add remaining dry ingredients and spoon into muffin tins. Bake at 400 degrees F for twenty minutes.

Recipe Totals: 2,238 calories, 398 g carbohydrates (17 g dietary fiber and 220 g sugars), 387 mg cholesterol, 63 g total fat (35 g saturated fat), 43 g protein, 2,531 mg sodium.
Dietary Exchanges (recipe totals): Bread, 10.5; Fat, 8.57; Fruit, 13; Lean Meat, 1.1; Milk, 1.1; Vegetables, 0.
Remember to divide totals by the number of servings.

Raisin Oatmeal Scones

Servings: Makes ten to twelve scones. Serves six.

My family claims I put oatmeal in everything I make. I don't, but I'm sure it can make most breads better. These scones are wonderful. I like to use golden raisins, but currants, blueberries, cherries, or just regular raisins are equally good.

Ingredients	All-Dry
1 cup enriched flour	1 cup
¼ cup white granulated sugar	¼ cup
1 teaspoon double-acting baking powder	1 teaspoon
¼ teaspoon salt	¼ teaspoon
2 ounces butter	¼ cup shortening powder
¼ teaspoon baking soda	¼ teaspoon
¾ cup dry rolled oats	¾ cup
½ cup packed golden seedless raisins	½ cup
½ cup cultured buttermilk	⅙ cup powder
nil water	¾ cup

Instructions: Combine sugar and butter. Add remaining ingredients and turn out on a floured pastry sheet. Knead for two to three minutes until smooth. Shape into a round and score it into six wedges. Place on greased baking sheet, sprinkle top with extra granular sugar, and bake at 400 degrees F for twenty minutes or until lightly browned.

Recipe Totals: 1,582 calories, 260 g carbohydrates (13 g dietary fiber and 121 g sugars), 128 mg cholesterol, 53 g total fat (30 g saturated fat), 30 g protein, 1,947 mg sodium.

Dietary Exchanges (recipe totals): Bread, 7.78; Fat, 9.07; Fruit, 7.25; Lean Meat, 0; Milk, 0.551; Vegetables, 0.

Remember to divide totals by the number of servings.

Scottish Crumpets

Servings: Makes twelve crumpets. Serves six.

These crumpets are more like a rich scone, or party biscuit, baked on a griddle (called a girdle in Scotland). They melt in your mouth when you eat them with blackberry jam and fresh butter. They make a wonderful breakfast accompaniment or a special snack.

Ingredients	All-Dry
3 cups enriched flour	3 cups
1 tablespoon double-acting baking powder	1 tablespoon
2 tablespoons white granulated sugar	2 tablespoons
2 tablespoons butter	2 tablespoons shortening powder
1 raw whole egg, extra-large	2 tablespoons powder
1 cup whole milk	⅓ cup powder
½ teaspoon salt	½ teaspoon
nil water	1⅓ cups

Instructions: Mix all dry ingredients together, then cut in the butter. Make a well in the dry ingredients and put in the egg and half the milk. With a fork, whip the egg and milk together, then gradually mix in the dry ingredients. Add more milk as necessary, just until you have a stiff but moist dough. Fry by the spoonful on a hot griddle, turning when bubbles appear over the surface. Serve hot.

Note: I like to use more sugar and butter in mine, then serve them plain or sprinkled with powdered sugar. I use about a half-cup each of sugar and butter. Using a heat diffuser will even and slow the cooking process, so the crumpets do not burn.

Recipe Totals: 1,882 calories, 330 g carbohydrates (12 g dietary fiber and 44 g sugars), 342 mg cholesterol, 41 g total fat (21 g saturated fat), 53 g protein, 2,959 mg sodium.

Dietary Exchanges (recipe totals): Bread, 16.9; Fat, 6.62; Fruit, 1.63; Lean Meat, 1.1; Milk, 1; Vegetables, 0.

Remember to divide totals by the number of servings.

Scottish Oat Cakes

Servings: Makes forty-eight. Serves 24.

This recipe was given to King Arthur Flour by Margaret and Lillian Sticht, of Connecticut. The Stichts say, "These oat cakes don't look like much but are truly love at first bite." They are a cross between a cracker and a flatbread.

Ingredients	All–Dry
3 cups multipurpose white wheat flour	3 cups
3 cups dry rolled oats	3 cups
1 cup (2 sticks)butter	1 cup butter powder
1 cup (1 stick) vegetable shortening	1 cup powder
1 cup white granulated sugar	1 cup
½ teaspoon salt	½ teaspoon
¼ cup water	1¼ cups

Instructions: Mix all the dry ingredients with two sticks of butter and one stick of vegetable shortening. Blend well. Gradually add water. Form into a ball. Divide the dough into four pieces. Roll each piece out between two sheets of waxed paper until about a quarter-inch thick. Cut the dough into rectangles of about two inches by three inches, and place on an ungreased cookie sheet. Bake for fifteen to twenty minutes in an oven preheated to 350 degrees F. (Incidentally, these could also be cooked in your skillet using a heat diffuser and low heat.)

(RECIPE COURTESY OF KING ARTHUR FLOUR)

Recipe Totals: 6,264 calories, 614 g carbohydrates (64 g dietary fiber and 217 g sugars), 497 mg cholesterol, 410 g total fat (170 g saturated fat), 85 g protein, 2,965 mg sodium.

Dietary Exchanges (recipe totals): Bread, 8.61; Fat, 76.2; Fruit, 13; Lean Meat, 0; Milk, 0; Vegetables, 0.

Remember to divide totals by the number of servings.

Singing Hinnies (Fried Cakes)

Servings: Makes eight cakes. Serves four.

These cakes get their strange name from the fact that they're cooked in an open skillet. As the butter and cream begins to melt on the bottom of the cakes it sizzles as though it were singing. My father was born in Aberdeen, Scotland, and came to the U.S. as a child. This is a good Scottish recipe that we enjoy. I hope you will too. Incidentally, these cakes go well with kippered herring and scrambled eggs.

Ingredients	All-Dry
1½ cups enriched flour	1½ cups
½ cup unsalted butter	½ cup shortening powder
½ cup dried currants	½ cup
1 teaspoon double-acting baking powder	1 teaspoon
½ teaspoon salt	½ teaspoon
¼ cup white granulated sugar	¼ cup
⅔ cup cultured buttermilk	⅓ cup powder
⅛ teaspoon baking soda	⅛ teaspoon
nil water	¾ cup

Instructions: Mix dry ingredients, then work in butter until crumbly. Add buttermilk to make a soft dough. Roll out, cut out cakes two inches in diameter, and bake on both sides in a hot skillet.

Note: These will not sizzle if you use dry shortening powder and buttermilk, as they do with fresh, but they still taste great. I mix all of the dry ingredients in a plastic bag. When I'm ready to make them, I just add the water to the plastic bag and knead. Once the mixture has formed a dough, I usually just use a little mayonnaise (single-portion packs work great) to grease my pan, and I turn the whole ball of dough out of the bag into the pan. As I turn the dough out, I pull the bag back over my hand and pat the dough very thin so it will cook quickly. I turn the stove on and sizzle the dough on one side. Next, I cut it in quarters, and flip them over to cook. When done, I cut it into wedges. They don't look as nice this way, but they are just as good.

Recipe Totals: 2,065 calories, 288 g carbohydrates (14 g dietary fiber and 137 g sugars), 254 mg cholesterol, 96 g total fat (58 g saturated fat), 30 g protein, 1,906 mg sodium.

Dietary Exchanges (recipe totals): Bread, 8.44; Fat, 23.9; Fruit, 7.98; Lean Meat, 0; Milk, 0.735; Vegetables, 0.

Remember to divide totals by the number of servings.

Steamed Berry Bread

Servings: Makes one loaf. Serves four.

This bread is full of flavor. I like to use dried cranberries instead of the strawberries.

Ingredients	All-Dry
½ cup medium-sized orange	¼ cup freeze-dried
¼ cup packed brown sugar	¼ cup
¼ cup chopped, dried English walnuts	¼ cup
1 raw whole egg, extra-large	2 tablespoons powder
2 tablespoons olive oil	2 tablespoons shortening powder
1 cup fresh, sliced strawberries	½ cup
1½ cups dry, sweet-corn muffin mix	1½ cups (box Jiffy)
3 cups water	4¾ cups

Instructions: Grate one tablespoon of orange rind. (Peel white rind off and discard.) Remove all seeds. Mince orange up finely. Combine orange rind and minced pulp with brown sugar. Add egg, finely chopped nuts, oil, and chopped strawberries. In a greased casserole dish, alternate layers of fruit mixture and dry muffin mix. Using a knife or fork, cut through mixture a number of times to moisten the dry mix. Cover casserole with greased aluminum foil and secure. Put rack and three cups of water in a four- or six-quart pressure cooker. Place dish on rack. Do not put the pressure regulator on. Heat until steam flows gently from the vent pipe. Cook for ten minutes. Place the pressure regulator on, and cook for another thirty-five minutes at fifteen pounds pressure. After cooking, let pressure subside as cooker cools down naturally. When pressure is down, remove bread and let cool. Note: These instructions have been changed to accommodate a baker not working in a home kitchen.

(RECIPE COURTESY OF NATIONAL PRESTO IND.)

Recipe Totals: 1,733 calories, 241 g carbohydrates (5 g dietary fiber and 70 g sugars), 247 mg cholesterol, 78 g total fat (7 g saturated fat), 25 g protein, 1,460 mg sodium.

Dietary Exchanges (recipe totals): Bread, 4.84; Fat, 10.4; Fruit, 10.7; Lean Meat, 1.1; Milk, 0; Vegetables, 0.

Remember to divide totals by the number of servings

Welsh Tea Bread (Bara-Brith)

Servings: Makes one loaf. Serves six to eight.

This tea bread is terrific at any time of the day. I like to toast it for breakfast, but it's great as a dessert also. Don't hesitate to try some of your flavored and herbal teas in place of regular tea.

Ingredients	All-Dry
2½ cups enriched flour	2½ cups
1 teaspoon ground allspice	1 teaspoon
1 teaspoon double-acting baking powder	1 teaspoon
1 cup tea brewed with distilled water	1 teaspoon instant tea
1 tablespoon fresh lemon juice	½ teaspoon powder
1 cup packed brown sugar	1 cup
1½ cups packed golden seedless raisins	1½ cups
1 raw whole egg, extra-large	2 tablespoons powder
½ cup butter oil (ghee)	½ cup shortening powder
nil water	1½ cups

Instructions: Add spice and fruit to tea to soak. Set aside. Combine sugar, egg, and butter. Add remaining ingredients, then add fruit and tea mixture. Pour into a greased and floured loaf pan and bake at 325 degrees F for ninety minutes or until done.

Recipe Totals: 3,688 calories, 657 g carbohydrates (19 g dietary fiber and 409 g sugars), 509 mg cholesterol, 112 g total fat (66 g saturated fat), 47 g protein, 680 mg sodium.
Dietary Exchanges (recipe totals): Bread, 14.1; Fat, 16.6; Fruit, 25.8; Lean Meat, 1.1; Milk, 0; Vegetables, 0.
Remember to divide totals by the number of servings.

Shortbread Scones

Servings: Makes six large scones. Serves six.

These are traditional Scottish shortbread scones. They're exceptionally rich and have a mellow flavor. They are high in fat, but if you make them crisp they'll keep well, and they'll be great for those days when you are really burning up the calories. They also make a nice dessert scone with tea or coffee.

Ingredients	All-Dry
8 ounces (two sticks) unsalted butter	1 cup shortening powder
2 cups enriched flour	2 cups
¼ teaspoon double-acting baking powder	¼ teaspoon
1 cup white granulated sugar	1 cup
1 raw whole egg, extra-large	2 tablespoons powder
nil water	1 cup

Instructions: Have butter at room temperature. Put flour, baking powder, and sugar in a bowl or pan and stir to blend. Work butter into dry ingredients. Beat egg and reserve one tablespoonful. Add egg to mixture. Blend to form a soft dough. Shape into a round, and pat out to a half-inch thick. Score into six wedges. Brush top with remaining egg and sprinkle with extra sugar. Bake at 375 degrees F for thirty minutes or until light brown.

Recipe Totals: 3,382 calories, 394 g carbohydrates (8 g dietary fiber and 205 g sugars), 744 mg cholesterol, 192 g total fat (116 g saturated fat), 34 g protein, 589 mg sodium.

Dietary Exchanges (recipe totals): Bread, 11.3; Fat, 48.4; Fruit, 13; Lean Meat, 1.1; Milk, 13; Vegetables, 0.

Remember to divide totals by the number of servings.

Spiced Tea Biscuits

Servings: Makes twelve biscuits. Serves six.

This is a slightly sweet biscuit with just enough sugar to perk you up in the middle of the afternoon when you need a little something to keep you going.

Ingredients	All-Dry
1⅓ cups enriched flour	1⅓ cups
¼ teaspoon salt	¼ teaspoon
⅓ cup olive oil	⅓ cup shortening powder
1 teaspoon pure vanilla extract	½ teaspoon powder
⅓ cup white granulated sugar	⅓ cup
⅛ teaspoon ground nutmeg	⅛ teaspoon
¾ cup whole milk	¼ cup powder
2 teaspoons double-acting baking powder	2 teaspoons
nil water	1¼ cups

(continued)

Instructions: Mix oil and sugar. Add all other ingredients and blend well. Drop by spoonfuls and flatten with a fork. Sprinkle tops with granular sugar. Bake at 375 degrees F for fifteen minutes.

Recipe Totals: 1,617 calories, 206 g carbohydrates (6 g dietary fiber and 78 g sugars), 25 mg cholesterol, 80 g total fat (14 g saturated fat), 23 g protein, 1,600 sodium.

Dietary Exchanges (recipe totals): Bread, 7.51; Fat, 15.1; Fruit, 4.33; Lean Meat, 0; Milk, 0.75; Vegetables, 0.

Remember to divide totals by the number of servings.

Seven-Up Bread

Servings: Makes one loaf. Serves eight.

This is a recipe given to me by a friend. You can accentuate the lemon-lime flavor of the Seven-Up by using lemon extract instead of vanilla. Lemon-flavored powdered sugar is nice just sprinkled sparingly on top.

Ingredients	All-Dry
1 cup Seven-Up soda pop	1 tablespoon powdered lemonade
1 raw whole egg, extra-large	2 tablespoons powder
1 tablespoon pure vanilla extract	nil
⅛ teaspoon ground nutmeg	⅛ teaspoon
¾ cup white granulated sugar	¾ cup
2⅔ cups biscuit mix	2⅓ cups
nil water (carbonated if available)	1¼ cups

Instructions: Combine egg and sugar, then add vanilla and nutmeg. Alternately add biscuit mix and Seven-Up. Bake in a greased and floured loaf pan for fifty minutes at 375 degrees F.

Recipe Totals: 2,662 calories, 453 g carbohydrates (0.1 g dietary fiber and 151 g sugars), 247 mg cholesterol, 74 g total fat (20 g saturated fat), 44 g protein, 5,761 mg sodium.

Dietary Exchanges (recipe totals): Bread, 0.01; Fat, 0.598; Fruit, 11.2; Lean Meat, 1.1; Milk, 0; Vegetables, 0.

Remember to divide totals by the number of servings.

* CHAPTER 6 *
Quick Desserts

There are never too many recipes for desserts and other sweets, as far as I am concerned. I know there must be others like me in this ol' world because of the abundance of cookbooks devoted entirely to the topic of desserts, or individual types of sweets, such as *The Cake Bible, All About Pies, The Best Tortes Ever,* and probably thousands of others.

Even with the profusion of cookbooks, I'm still happy to come across any cookbook that has even one or two recipes that are new to me. I especially love the old cookbooks published before the 1940s. So if you've got any like that, don't throw them out. Just write to me: I'll probably want them.

Desserts are part of my childhood memory, recalling the times when meals were endured only because of the promise of better to come, because of the anticipation of that wonderful, rich, luscious treat that punctuated the end of the meal.

No meal seems complete to me without dessert, or some small sweet item. It doesn't have to be something elaborate. It can be a piece of fruit, a cookie, or sometimes, on the go, a small piece of hard candy.

The dessert breads, cakes, and cookies I've given you here cover a wide range of ingredients and flavor variations. I've tried to cover items that will work for you on a boat or out on the trail. There are desserts that are light and delicate, and there are some that are sinfully rich and gooey. I've done my best to include items that will appeal to everyone.

I've intentionally not specified pan sizes for any of the following recipes because of the wide variety of baking devices available. A good rule of thumb is to never fill your pan more than halfway with batter.

Apple Brownies

Servings: Makes twelve to sixteen brownies. Serves twelve.

These bars are moist and delicious. Try them for lunch with a chunk of Cheddar cheese. You can vary this recipe simply by using different fruit. Another option is to cut the sugar down to a quarter-cup, and bake it as a dinner bread.

Ingredients	All-Dry
½ cup butter oil (ghee)	½ cup shortening powder
1 cup white granulated sugar	1 cup
1 raw whole egg, extra-large	2 tablespoons powder
½ cup chopped dried English walnuts	½ cup
2 cups peeled apple slices	1 cup dried
¼ teaspoon salt	¼ teaspoon
1 cup enriched flour	1 cup
½ teaspoon double-acting baking powder	½ teaspoon
½ teaspoon baking soda	½ teaspoon
¼ teaspoon cinnamon	¼ teaspoon
nil water	1¾ cups, boiling

Instructions: Combine sugar, butter and egg. Add all other ingredients and blend well. Bake at 350 degrees F for forty minutes.

Note: If you're using dried fruit, cover it with boiling water and let it stand for ten minutes or until cool, then add to dry ingredients, including the liquid.

Recipe Totals: 2,718 calories, 341.4 g carbohydrates (11 g dietary fiber and 231 g sugars), 509 mg cholesterol, 147 g total fat (69 g saturated fat), 29 g protein, 1,491 mg sodium.

Dietary Exchanges (recipe totals): Bread, 6.23; Fat, 16.6; Fruit, 14.7; Lean Meat, 1.1; Milk, 0; Vegetables, 0.

Remember to divide totals by the number of servings.

Apple Whole-Wheat Bread Pudding

Servings: Makes six servings.

I love bread pudding. This moist and delicious recipe is fairly quick to make, and can really perk up an otherwise drab meal.

Ingredients

	All-Dry
8 slices whole-wheat bread	2⅔ cups croutons
⅓ cup packed golden seedless raisins	⅓ cup
1¼ cups whole milk	½ cup powder
½ cup apple butter	¼ cup apple powder
2 raw whole eggs, extra-large	4 tablespoons powder
2 tablespoons white granulated sugar	⅛ cup
1 teaspoon pure vanilla extract	½ teaspoon powder
½ teaspoon salt	½ teaspoon
½ teaspoon cinnamon	½ teaspoon
¼ teaspoon ground nutmeg	¼ teaspoon
2 cups water	4¼ cups
2 cups vanilla ice cream	instant pudding— see below

Instructions: Combine all ingredients except water and ice cream. Let stand for twenty minutes to soften bread. Stir, then spoon into a greased one-quart casserole dish or bowl. Cover bowl securely with greased aluminum foil. Put two cups of water and a rack in pressure cooker. Place bowl on rack. Place pressure regulator on vent pipe and cook for twenty-five minutes at fifteen pounds of pressure. Cool cooker at once. Serve hot.

Note: They serve this with ice cream, but unless you are in an area with pristine snow where you can make snow ice cream, this suggestion is impossible. I recommend mixing one small pack of vanilla instant pudding, one-third cup powdered milk, and two-and-a-half cups of cold water for a vanilla creme sauce.

(Recipe courtesy of National Presto Ind.)

Recipe Totals: 2,177 calories, 344 g carbohydrates (22 g dietary fiber and 220 g sugars), 652 mg cholesterol, 64 g total fat (31 g saturated fat), 63 g protein, 3,054 mg sodium.

Dietary Exchanges (recipe totals): Bread, 8.41; Fat, 8.7; Fruit, 11.4; Lean Meat, 2.21; Milk, 2.57; Vegetables, 0.

Remember to divide totals by the number of servings.

Applesauce Cake

Servings: Makes sixteen squares. Serves sixteen.

This is a very moist cake. It's as good at the breakfast table as it is for dessert. If you are trying to cut back on fat, leave the margarine out. You won't even miss it because applesauce works well as a fat replacement in cakes and sweet muffins. If you have this cake for breakfast, you might want to put a streusel top on it. If you want to use it for dessert, try melting some caramels with one or two tablespoons of milk and drizzling it over the top. I like the caramel topping with ice cream too.

Ingredients	All–Dry
1 cup white granulated sugar	1 cup
1 teaspoon baking soda	1 teaspoon
1 teaspoon cinnamon	1 teaspoon
⅛ teaspoon salt	⅛ teaspoon
1 cup enriched, all-purpose white flour	1 cup
1 raw whole egg, extra-large	2 tablespoons powder
1 stick (½ cup) unsalted margarine	½ cup shortening powder
16 ounces (2 cups) canned sweetened applesauce	¾ cup powdered apple
nil water	2⅓ cups

Instructions: Combine sugar and margarine. Add egg and beat well. Add all other ingredients and beat until smooth. Bake in a greased, floured pan for twenty-five minutes at 350 degrees F.

Note: When you're using the all-dry ingredients, combine the apple powder with the water and set aside for three to five minutes to rehydrate into applesauce. This will ensure a smoother batter and a better flavor.

Recipe Totals: 2,476 calories, 389 g carbohydrates (11 g dietary fiber and 288 g sugars), 247 mg cholesterol, 99 g total fat (19 g saturated fat), 22 g protein, 1,622 mg sodium.

Dietary Exchanges (recipe totals): Bread, 5.66; Fat, 18.7; Fruit, 18.4; Lean Meat, 1.1; Milk, 0; Vegetables, 0.

Remember to divide totals by the number of servings.

Baked Applesauce Pudding

Servings: Makes six servings

This dessert is very easy to make, and falls into the category of comfort food. I like it without the applesauce, too. It may not sound glamorous, but you won't find a better dessert. My mother used leftover biscuits to make a similar dessert and called it Poor Man's Pie.

Ingredients	All-Dry
8 slices soft white bread	2⅔ cups croutons
16 ounces canned sweetened applesauce	¾ cup powdered apple
⅓ cup unpacked seedless raisins	⅓ cup
½ teaspoon cinnamon	½ teaspoon
¼ cup packed brown sugar	¼ cup
2 raw whole eggs, extra-large	4 tablespoons powder
2½ cups 2 percent low-fat milk with vitamin A	¾ cup powder
½ teaspoon pure vanilla extract	⅛ teaspoon vanilla powder
¼ teaspoon salt	¼ teaspoon
¼ cup packed brown sugar	¼ cup
¼ cup butter	¼ cup powder
nil water	5 cups

Instructions: Spread bread slices with butter. Put four slices of bread, buttered side up, in baking dish. Mix applesauce, raisins, cinnamon, and quarter-cup of brown sugar, then pour over the bread in baking dish. Cut remaining four bread slices into triangles and place on top of mixture. Beat eggs, milk, vanilla, salt, and remaining quarter-cup brown sugar. Pour over all. Sprinkle with extra cinnamon if desired. Bake at 350 degrees F for forty to fifty minutes.

Note: When you're using all-dry ingredients, combine apple powder and butter powder with two cups of the water, and let rehydrate for three to five minutes before blending with other ingredients. It will make a smoother mixture that will taste better.

Recipe Totals: 2,469 calories, 398 g carbohydrates (13 dietary fiber and 285 g sugars), 671 mg cholesterol, 78 g total fat (41 g saturated fat), 58 g protein, 2,667 mg sodium.

Dietary Exchanges (recipe totals): Bread, 7.64; Fat, 12.7; Fruit, 15.6; Lean Meat, 2.21; Milk, 2.5; Vegetables, 0.

Remember to divide totals by the number of servings.

Butterscotch Brownies

Servings: Makes twenty-four brownies. Serves twenty-four.

This bread packs a real load of calories into a small bar. It's great for those days when you know you will be expending lots of energy. If you leave out most of the sugar and increase the coconut to one cup, it is a great bread to have with curry dishes. The coconut adds a nice flavor that really complements spicy dishes. I love this recipe, but I don't fix it at home except on holidays. It is also great made in a loaf form and toasted for breakfast—but then, I like pie for breakfast, too. Did I mention that I have a sweet tooth? Or should I say teeth?

Ingredients	All-Dry
½ cup butter oil (ghee)	½ cup shortening powder
2 cups packed brown sugar	2 cups
2 raw whole eggs, extra-large	4 tablespoons powder
1 teaspoon salt	1 teaspoon
1½ cups enriched flour	1½ cups
1 teaspoon double-acting baking powder	1 teaspoon
1 teaspoon pure vanilla extract	¹⁄₁₆ teaspoon vanilla powder
1 cup chopped dried English walnuts	1 cup
½ cup dried, sweetened, shredded coconut	½ cup
nil water	1⅛ cups

Instructions: Combine butter, brown sugar, and eggs. Add remaining ingredients and blend well. Spread in a greased, floured baking pan, and bake at 350 degrees F for twenty-five minutes.

Recipe Totals: 4,407 calories, 619 g carbohydrates (14 g dietary fiber and 455 g sugars), 756 mg cholesterol, 206 g total fat (88 g saturated fat), 52 g protein, 3,073 mg sodium.

Dietary Exchanges (recipe totals): Bread, 9.64; Fat, 19.6; Fruit, 28.9; Lean Meat, 2.21; Milk, 0; Vegetables, 0.

Remember to divide totals by the number of servings.

Crumb Cake

Servings: Makes two dozen squares. Serves twelve to twenty-four.

The first Crumb Cake I remember having was on a visit to my brother's house in New York. My sister-in-law bought an Entenmann Crumb Cake at the deli. It was wonderful. It was also a long time before Entenmann's cakes made it into our southern stores. It was still good when I tried it, but not as good as that first one in New York. The newness of it then made it special. This recipe is a fairly simple one, but offers a very rich flavor. I love this with a hot cup of coffee or tea.

Ingredients	All-Dry
1½ cups packed brown sugar	1½ cups
½ cup unsalted margarine	⅓ cup butter powder or shortening
1 teaspoon pure vanilla extract	½ teaspoon powder
2 cups all-purpose enriched white flour	2 cups
1 cup cultured buttermilk	⅓ cup powder
1 teaspoon baking soda	1 teaspoon
¼ teaspoon cream of tartar	¼ teaspoon
nil water	1½ cups

Instructions: Combine sugar, flour, and butter together until crumbly. Reserve one cup of crumbs for the topping. Mix all other ingredients together and pour into a greased pan, top with reserved crumbs, and bake at 325 degrees F for thirty minutes.

Recipe Totals: 3,071 calories, 526 g carbohydrates (8 g dietary fiber and 338 g sugars), 9 mg cholesterol, 96 g total fat (19 g saturated fat), 35 g protein, 1,655 mg sodium.

Dietary Exchanges (recipe totals): Bread, 11.3; Fat, 18.2; Fruit, 20.5; Lean Meat, 0; Milk, 1.1; Vegetables, 0.

Remember to divide totals by the number of servings.

Chocolate Fudge Cake

Servings: Makes eight servings.

This is similar to the Chocolate Dream Fudge Cake, but not as chocolatey. This version is for those who try to remain sensible about what they eat.

Ingredients	All-Dry
1 cup enriched flour	1 cup
¾ cup toasted wheat germ	¾ cup
¾ cup white granulated sugar	¾ cup
2 teaspoons double-acting baking powder	2 teaspoons
¼ teaspoon salt	¼ teaspoon
2 tablespoons butter oil (ghee)	2 tablespoons shortening powder
⅔ cup whole milk	¼ cup powder
1 teaspoon pure vanilla extract	1 teaspoon powder
1 cup packed brown sugar	1 cup
½ cup non-alkalized natural cocoa powder	½ cup
2 cups hot water	2¾ cups

Instructions: Reserve brown sugar and cocoa powder. Mix all other ingredients except water and pour into a greased pan. Sprinkle cocoa and brown sugar over batter. Pour hot water over all, and bake for forty minutes at 375 degrees F.

Recipe Totals: 2,599 calories, 533 g carbohydrates (28 g dietary fiber and 384 g sugars), 88 mg cholesterol, 46 g total fat (21 g saturated fat), 52 g protein, 1,697 mg sodium.

Dietary Exchanges (recipe totals): Bread, 8.63; Fat, 5; Fruit, 23.4; Lean Meat, 1.69; Milk, 0.667; Vegetables, 0.

Remember to divide totals by the number of servings.

Chocolate Dream Hot Fudge Cake

Servings: Makes six to eight servings.

This fudge cake is so rich you can almost feel it marching to your waistline—but it's *heavenly.* If you can round up some vanilla ice cream as well, this is what sweet dreams are made of.

Ingredients	All-Dry
1⅔ cups biscuit mix	1⅔ cups
6 ounces semisweet chocolate chips	1 cup
½ cup white granulated sugar	½ cup
½ cup whole milk	⅛ cup powder
½ cup chopped dried pecans	½ cup
¼ cup non-alkalized natural cocoa powder	¼ cup
½ cup packed brown sugar	½ cup
1½ cups boiling water	2 cups

Instructions: Pour boiling water over chocolate chips and set aside. Reserve brown sugar. Mix all other ingredients together and pour in a deep buttered pan. Sprinkle brown sugar on top. Pour chocolate chips and water over batter. Bake for forty minutes at 375 degrees F.

Recipe Totals: 3,290 calories, 515 g carbohydrates (19 g dietary fiber and 309 g sugars), 17 mg cholesterol, 140 g total fat (47 g saturated fat), 43 g protein, 3,860 mg sodium.

Dietary Exchanges (recipe totals): Bread, 2.01; Fat, 15.9; Fruit, 19; Lean Meat, 0.551; Milk, 0.5; Vegetables, 0.

Remember to divide totals by the number of servings.

Cinnamon Pudding Cake

Servings: Makes eight servings.

Please be forewarned: According to a recent news item, the smell of cinnamon makes men amorous. While I can't vouch for the truth of that, I do know they'll enjoy this cinnamon pudding cake. And women will, also—I know I do.

Ingredients	All-Dry
2 cups enriched flour	2 cups
1 cup white granulated sugar	1 cup
1 cup whole milk	⅓ cup powder
⅓ cup butter oil (ghee)	⅓ cup shortening powder
2 teaspoons double-acting baking powder	2 teaspoons
2 teaspoons cinnamon	2 teaspoons
½ cup chopped dried English walnuts	½ cup
2 cups packed brown sugar	2 cups
1½ cups boiling water	2¾ cups

(continued)

Instructions: Mix one-and-a-half cups of boiling water with three tablespoons butter and two cups of brown sugar. Set aside. Mix flour, sugar, milk, baking powder, cinnamon, and two table-spoons butter. Pour batter into a ten-inch buttered Duth oven, sprinkle with nuts. Pour brown-sugar-and-water mixture over all, and bake at 350 degrees F for forty minutes.

Recipe Totals: 4,432 calories, 849 g carbohydrates (13 g dietary fiber and 645 g sugars), 197 mg cholesterol, 112 g total fat (48 g saturated fat), 42 g protein, 1,278 mg sodium.
Dietary Exchanges (recipe totals): Bread, 11.9; Fat, 11.5; Fruit, 40.4; Lean Meat, 0; Milk, 1; Vegetables, 0.
Remember to divide totals by the number of servings.

Lemon Bars

Servings: Makes twelve bars.

This is the lemon version of a brownie. I find them especially refreshing in the summertime. I guess it's the summertime lemonade thing—but don't try to drink lemonade *and* eat these. You might end up with a permanent pucker.

Ingredients	All-Dry
½ cup unsalted butter	⅓ cup powder
1 cup white granulated sugar	1 cup
2 raw whole eggs, extra-large	4 tablespoons powder
5 tablespoons bottled lemon juice	1 tablespoon lemon powder
⅔ cup enriched flour	⅔ cup
nil water	1 cup

Instructions: Combine butter and sugar. Add eggs and beat well. Add all other ingredients and beat until smooth. Pour into a greased and floured nine-inch pan. Bake at 325 degrees F for twenty-five minutes.

Recipe Totals: 2,075 calories, 271 g carbohydrates (3 g dietary fiber and 207 g sugars), 742 mg cholesterol, 105 g total fat (61 g saturated fat), 24 g protein, 177 mg sodium.
Dietary Exchanges (recipe totals): Bread, 3.77; Fat, 25.1; Fruit, 13.3; Lean Meat, 2.21; Milk, 0; Vegetables, 0.
Remember to divide totals by the number of servings.

French Mocha Cake

Servings: Makes six servings.

My family loves chocolate, and we like coffee, too, so this is a perfect blend for us. I hope you will enjoy it also. This makes one layer, but what a decadent layer it is!

Ingredients	All-Dry
¼ cup unsalted butter	¼ cup shortening powder
1 cup packed brown sugar	1 cup
1 raw whole egg, extra-large	2 tablespoons powder
2 cups prepared biscuit mix	2 cups
1 teaspoon instant dry cappuccino coffee	1 teaspoon
1 cup water (hot)	1¾ cup (hot)

Instructions: Combine all ingredients but water. Blend well. Add one cup hot water. Pour batter into a greased and floured pan. Bake for thirty minutes at 350 degrees F.

Frosting option: Put about one-third cup of small, semi-sweet chocolate chips on top of the hot cake and cover for approximately forty-five seconds. The heat from the cake will melt the chips and they can then be spread over the top of the cake into a nice glaze.

Note: If you want more of a mocha flavor, try adding hot coffee instead of the water.

Recipe Totals: 2,116 calories, 307 g carbohydrates (6 g dietary fiber and 176 g sugars), 383 mg cholesterol, 88 g total fat (39 g saturated fat), 29 g protein, 2,984 mg sodium.

Dietary Exchanges (recipe totals): Bread, 8.88; Fat, 18.5; Fruit, 10.4; Lean Meat, 1.1; Milk, 0; Vegetables, 0.

Remember to divide totals by the number of servings.

Lemon Crunch Cake

Servings: Makes six to eight servings.

This cake has a streusel-like topping when done. I like to use Total cereal in any recipe calling for cereal because of the extra vitamins. This topping also works well for a quick coffee cake, using one and one-half cups of biscuit mix and one cup of sugar instead of the cake mix. You can vary this recipe endlessly with different cake mixes, nuts, spices, fruit, and so on. I like to divide the recipe in half and use the new small cake mixes that are on the market now. They are perfect for two to four people.

Ingredients	All-Dry
2½ cups lemon cake mix	2½ cups
2 raw whole eggs, extra-large	4 tablespoons powder
⅓ cup olive oil	⅓ cup powdered butter
1 cup whole milk	⅓ cup powder
1 cup packed brown sugar	1 cup
½ cup butter oil (ghee)	½ cup powdered butter
1 cup cereal, corn flakes	1 cup
nil water	2⅓ cups

Instructions: Melt butter oil in skillet. (One quarter-pound stick of butter may be substituted for butter oil.) Remove from heat. Evenly distribute brown sugar, then corn flakes. Mix cake according to package, and pour over all. Bake at 350 degrees F for twenty-five minutes.

Note: If you're using the all-dry ingredients, combine the half-cup of butter powder with brown sugar. Sprinkle mixture over the bottom of the skillet, then sprinkle one-third cup of water over brown sugar mixture. Use remaining water to mix with cake mix, and pour batter over all. Bake as above.

Recipe Totals: 4,742 calories, 574 g carbohydrates (2 g dietary fiber and 229 g sugars), 928 mg cholesterol, 256 g total fat (106 g saturated fat), 51 g protein, 3,671 mg sodium.

Dietary Exchanges (recipe totals): Bread, 10.1; Fat, 45; Fruit, 25.4; Lean Meat, 2.21; Milk, 1; Vegetables, 0.

Remember to divide totals by the number of servings.

Graham Cracker Cake

Servings: Makes eight to twelve servings.

I always loved graham crackers, and still do, so this is a special favorite. This makes a very moist, delicious cake. It is good with or without the sweet sauce. It is similar to a bread pudding in consistency.

Ingredients	All-Dry
(1) Cake	
4 raw whole eggs, extra-large	8 tablespoons powder
1½ cups white granulated sugar	1½ cups
2 teaspoons pure vanilla extract	1 teaspoon powder
3 teaspoons double-acting baking powder	1 tablespoon
1 teaspoon salt	1 teaspoon
2 cups 2 percent milk with vitamin A	⅔ cup powder
1 pound (6 cups) graham cracker crumbs	1 pound (6 cups)
nil water	3 cups
(2) Sweet Sauce	
¼ cup butter oil (ghee)	¼ cup shortening powder
¾ cup white granulated sugar	¾ cup
1½ cups water	2 cups
2 tablespoons enriched flour	2 tablespoons
2 teaspoons pure vanilla extract	1 teaspoon powder

Instructions:

(1) **Cake:** Mix all dry ingredients together. Add milk and let stand for five minutes. Add eggs and beat well. Add vanilla. Line double boiler with parchment paper. Pour batter into double boiler and bake until a knife inserted in the center comes out clean. Serve with sweet sauce.

(2) **Sweet Sauce:** Mix all ingredients and bring to a boil. Serve.

Recipe Totals: 4,798 calories, 841 g carbohydrates (13 g dietary fiber and 691 g sugars), 1,156 mg cholesterol, 130 g total fat (56 g saturated fat), 78 g protein, 6,884 mg sodium.

Dietary Exchanges (recipe totals): Bread, 23.4; Fat, 14.6; Fruit, 29.3; Lean Meat, 4.42; Milk, 2; Vegetables, 0.

Remember to divide totals by the number of servings.

Margaret Christian Roderick's Special Prune Cake

Servings: Makes three layers. Serves twenty-four.

One day during lunch break in geology lab, Linda McAuliffe, a good friend of mine, gave me a piece of the cake she was eating. It was just about the best cake I had ever eaten. I asked her to see if Margaret, who had baked the cake, would send me the recipe; and she did.

At that time, Linda lived with Margaret and Tom Roderick while their son, Tommy, was in the air force. That was a year or so before I ever met them. Eventually, Linda and I took calculus together and I would go out to Margaret and Tom's and spend the night with her. We would study together for a test or have our other friend, Susan, who was a math major, tutor us in calculus.

During these visits, you would not meet a more gracious hostess and host than Margaret and Tom. More likely than not, Margaret would bake a prune cake if she knew I was coming over; and it was always wonderful.

Because I had always driven to Margaret and Tom's house from the opposite direction, when my husband and I bought a house in Snellville, I had no idea that it was only about a mile from Margaret and Tom's house, but I soon found out. I saw them almost every day or talked to them when I didn't see them. They took me into their home and hearts just as though I was their own daughter. As my husband traveled constantly, Margaret and Tom would call me and ask me to come for dinner almost every night, and everything was always wonderful.

Every time I told them I didn't want to wear out my welcome, Tom would tease me and say they would break my plate if I didn't come on down for dinner. I guess you can tell that I loved them both very much. They were family to me.

After I moved away, I missed them most of all even though we talked and saw each other periodically. Margaret became seriously ill and passed away some years ago, but I'm positive she's taking care of the angels. She is greatly missed by everyone who knew her because she was good to everyone.

I keep in touch with Tom, and visit when I can. He can cook a meal that would put most cooks to shame. He insists, "Margaret taught me." He still likes to tease me about breaking my plate if I don't visit, and I love him. He is family to me. He is still good to everyone he knows.

So you see there is a lot of history behind this cake, lots of happy times. I hope you make this cake, and share it often making your own happy memories. I think Margaret would like that, and Tom will too.

Ingredients	All-Dry
(1) Cake	
5 raw whole eggs, extra-large	⅝ cup powder
3 cups enriched flour	3 cups
2¼ cups white granulated sugar	2¼ cups
½ tablespoon vanilla powder	½ tablespoon
1½ cups vegetable oil	1 cup shortening powder
1½ cups cultured buttermilk	½ cup powder
1½ cups dried stewed prunes, with sugar but no pits	1 cup dried, plus 1 cup boiling water
1½ teaspoons cinnamon	1½ teaspoons
1½ teaspoons ground allspice	1½ teaspoons
1½ teaspoons baking soda	1½ teaspoons
1½ teaspoons ground nutmeg	1½ teaspoons
nil water	4¼ cups
(2) Frosting	
¾ cup butter	½ cup powder
1½ cups white granulated sugar	1½ cups
¾ cup cultured buttermilk	¼ cup powder
1 tablespoon light corn syrup	3 tablespoons powder
½ tablespoon vanilla powder	½ tablespoon
nil water	1¼ cups

Instructions:

(1) Cake: Place sugar, spices, soda, oil, and eggs in a large bowl and beat well. Add flour and buttermilk alternately until all is blended. Stir in prunes and vanilla and do not beat long. Pour into three, nine-inch cake pans that have been greased and floured on the bottom only. Bake at 325 degrees F for forty-five minutes.

Note: For ease of cooking when you're not in your home kitchen, I would cut this recipe by one third and bake it in a sheet cake pan or Dutch oven. If you do this, don't forget to cut the frosting recipe as well. For the all-dry recipe, soak the prunes in the boiling water, then use the liquid too.

(2) Frosting: In a four-quart pot, melt one-and-a-half sticks butter, one-and-a-half cups sugar, three-quarter cup buttermilk, one tablespoon corn syrup, and one-half tablespoon vanilla. Bring mixture to a full boil, then remove from heat.

To frost the cake, lay a large piece of foil on a flat surface. Take one of the cake layers and place it on the foil. Pierce the cake all

(continued)

over with a knife. Spoon some of the frosting over the cake layer. It will run off, but keep putting it back on top of the cake. As the frosting cools on the cake, it will stick to the cake. Then place the second layer on top of the first layer and do the same as before with some of the frosting. When the frosting sticks to the second layer, put the third layer on the cake and follow the same procedure. If possible, chill after frosting.

Note: If you're following the all-dry recipe, pour one cup boiling water over the chopped prunes and allow to stand until cool. As you will use prunes and liquid, don't forget to subtract this cup of water from the total water for the mix.

Recipe Totals: 9,653 calories, 1,236 g carbohydrates (29 g dietary fiber and 913 g sugars), 1,627 mg cholesterol, 505 g total fat (137 g saturated fat), 98 g protein, 4,286 mg sodium.

Dietary Exchanges (recipe totals): Bread, 17; Fat, 94.4; Fruit, 49.7; Lean Meat, 5.52; Milk, 2.48; Vegetables, 0.

Remember to divide totals by the number of servings.

Orange Coconut Streusel

Servings: Makes two dozen squares. Serves twenty-four.

If you like ambrosia, you will like this cake. The orange slices make it very moist and delicious. Peeled fresh orange slices would be wonderful in this also. In fact, I can't think of a fruit that wouldn't be good.

Ingredients	All-Dry
1¾ cups enriched flour	1¾ cups
½ cup white granulated sugar	½ cup
½ cup olive oil	½ cup shortening powder
½ cup whole milk	⅙ cup powder
2 raw whole eggs, extra-large	4 tablespoons powder
2 teaspoons double-acting baking powder	2 teaspoons
2 cups canned mandarin oranges	See note below
1 cup sweetened flaked coconut	1 cup
¾ cup packed brown sugar	¾ cup
2 tablespoons butter oil (ghee)	2 tablespoons shortening powder
nil water	1¾ cups

Instructions, Streusel mixture: Combine three-quarter cup flour, three-quarter cup brown sugar, coconut and butter oil or shortening until crumbly. Set aside.

Combine white sugar, remaining flour, oil, oranges, baking powder, milk, and eggs. Beat well. Spread one half of batter in a greased and floured pan. Top with oranges and one-half of the streusel. Cover with remaining batter, with streusel on top. Bake at 350 degrees F for thirty to thirty-five minutes.

Note: Freeze-dried orange slices are not available, so substitute a half-cup of any dry fruit. Soak fruit in one cup of boiling water for approximately ten minutes. Drain, and use in place of orange slices as directed. You could also substitute one-half of a small pack of orange Jell-O.

Recipe Totals: 3,686 calories, 504 g carbohydrates (12 g dietary fiber and 331 g sugars), 576 mg cholesterol, 175 g total fat (58 g saturated fat), 45 g protein, 1,454 mg sodium.
Dietary Exchanges (recipe totals): Bread, 9.84; Fat, 31.4; Fruit, 21.6; Lean Meat, 2.21; Milk, 0.5; Vegetables, 0.
Remember to divide totals by the number of servings.

Orange Sponge Cake, Bush-Style

Servings: Makes twelve servings.

This recipe is from the *Cowboy Cookbook,* published by the Society for Range Management. It was submitted to them by John and Denial Mills, of Charleville, Queensland, Australia.

Ingredients

	All-Dry
8 raw whole eggs, extra-large	1 cup powder
1½ cups white granulated sugar	1½ cups
1½ cups enriched self-rising flour	1½ cups
½ cup cornstarch (corn flour)	½ cup
2 teaspoons cream of tartar	2 teaspoons
1 teaspoon baking soda	1 teaspoon
3 tablespoons grated fresh orange peel	1 tablespoon dried
nil water	2⅛ cups

Instructions: Mix together eggs, sugar, cream of tartar, and baking soda. With a knife, gently blend in orange peel, sifted flour and cornstarch. Grease and flour a cake tin or camp oven. Pour batter in, and cook at moderate temperature (approximately 325 to 350 degrees F) for twenty to thirty minutes.

Note: If using all-dry products, mix the eggs with sugar, cream of tartar, and soda. Keep egg mixture separate from flour mixture. When ready to make the cake, combine egg mixture with a small amount of water to make a smooth paste. Gradually add the water until all has been blended. A fork makes a good whisk substitute. Use the fork to whip the egg mixture until frothy, then mix as above.

(RECIPE COURTESY OF THE SOCIETY FOR RANGE MANAGEMENT)

Recipe Totals: 2,732 calories, 494 g carbohydrates (11 g dietary fiber and 309 g sugars), 1,977 mg cholesterol, 51 g total fat (15 g saturated fat), 81 g protein, 4,369 mg sodium.

Dietary Exchanges (recipe totals): Bread, 11; Fat, 4.65; Fruit, 19.8; Lean Meat, 8.84; Milk, 0; Vegetables, 0.

Remember to divide totals by the number of servings.

Ozark Pie

Servings: Makes one pie. Serves six.

Nancy and her husband, Jerry, invented the Sportsman Oven. They are extremely nice people. We had the chance to meet them a few years ago at one of the large Outdoor Expo shows. Nancy gave me this recipe, and said it was a favorite with her family and friends. It is a cross between a super-moist cake and a pie. It is excellent.

Ingredients	All-Dry
1 raw whole egg, extra-large	2 tablespoons powder
¾ cup white granulated sugar	¾ cup
1 teaspoon pure vanilla extract	¼ teaspoon powder
¼ cup enriched flour	¼ cup
1¼ teaspoons double-acting baking powder	1¼ teaspoons
½ medium apple with peel	1 cup dried
½ cup dry, roasted mixed nuts, unsalted (optional)	½ cup
nil water	1 cup

Instructions: Dice or slice apple, then place in a buttered pie dish or pan. Mix all other ingredients together, and pour over apples. Bake at 350 degrees F for twenty to twenty-five minutes.

Note: When you're using all-dry ingredients, use low-moisture dried apples, or reduce the quantity to a half-cup dried apples. Pour water over apples and allow to rehydrate for about five or ten minutes. Mix all other ingredients with apples and bake as above.

Recipe Totals: 1,238 calories, 204 g carbohydrates (9 g dietary fiber and 162 g sugars), 247 mg cholesterol, 42 g total fat (7 g saturated fat), 22 g protein, 694 mg sodium.

Dietary Exchanges (recipe totals): Bread, 1.41; Fat, 6.48; Fruit, 11.5; Lean Meat, 2.6; Milk, 0; Vegetables, 0.

Remember to divide totals by the number of servings.

Pecan Date Balls

Servings: Makes three dozen date balls. Serves eighteen.

I grew up with two huge pecan trees in our yard, and picking up pecans was a happy fall pastime. My mom had a large oak barrel in the pantry that we would usually more than fill with pecans. Sometimes at night we would shell a few pecans and sizzle them in butter on the small two-burner coal stove in our bedroom. It was heaven.

These cookies are good with or without the dates. They have just enough butter to toast the pecans as the cookie bakes, providing me with lots of memories and a taste of home.

Ingredients	All-Dry
1 cup butter	1 cup shortening powder
½ cup white granulated sugar	½ cup
2 teaspoons pure vanilla extract	1 teaspoon powder
2 cups enriched flour	2 cups
2 cups chopped dried pecans	2 cups
2 cups chopped dates	2 cups
¼ cup sifted white powdered sugar	¼ cup
nil water	½ cup

Instructions: Combine granular sugar, butter, vanilla, and flour. Add other ingredients. Roll teaspoonfuls of dough into balls and refrigerate (if possible) for ten minutes. Bake at 350 degrees F for twenty minutes. Remove from oven and roll in powdered sugar.

(see next page for recipe nutritional data)

Recipe Totals: 5,588 calories, 623 g carbohydrates (46 g dietary fiber and 374 g sugars), 497 mg cholesterol, 349 g total fat (128 g saturated fat), 53 g protein, 1,890 mg sodium.

Dietary Exchanges (recipe totals): Bread, 11.3; Fat, 64.9; Fruit, 26.9; Lean Meat, 2.2; Milk, 0; Vegetables, 0.

Remember to divide totals by the number of servings.

Steamed Chocolate Pudding Cake

Servings: Makes six servings.

This makes a wonderful chocolate pudding. Of course, I love chocolate. If you're not a chocaholic, I recommend you use an equal amount of butterscotch chips or peanut butter chips.

Ingredients	All-Dry
⅔ cup white granulated sugar	⅔ cup
3 tablespoons hard margarine or corn oil	3 tablespoons butter powder
1 raw whole egg, extra-large	2 tablespoons powder
½ cup cultured buttermilk	⅙ cup powder
½ teaspoon pure vanilla extract	¼ teaspoon powder
¾ cup enriched flour	¾ cup
¼ cup non-alkalized, natural cocoa powder	¼ cup
2 teaspoons double-acting baking powder	2 teaspoons
½ teaspoon baking soda	½ teaspoon
¼ teaspoon salt	¼ teaspoon
4 cups water	4¾ cups
⅛ cup sifted white powdered sugar (reserve)	⅛ cup

Instructions: Mix sugar, margarine, and then egg. Add buttermilk and vanilla. Add all other dry ingredients. Pour into a one-quart greased bowl or pan. Cover bowl securely with greased aluminum foil. Place cooking rack and four cups of water in a four- or six-quart pressure cooker. Put bowl on rack. Cover. Do not put pressure regulator on vent pipe. Heat until steam gently flows through vent pipe. Cook for one hour. Remove cake and let cool on wire rack for five minutes. Sprinkle with powdered sugar before serving.

(RECIPE COURTESY OF NATIONAL PRESTO IND.)

Recipe Totals: 1,474 calories, 259 g carbohydrates (21 g dietary fiber and 154 g sugars), 251 mg cholesterol, 49 g total fat (8 g saturated fat), 35 g protein, 2,766 mg sodium.

Dietary Exchanges (recipe totals): Bread, 4.22; Fat, 0.581; Fruit, 9.48; Lean Meat, 1.1; Milk, 0.551; Vegetables, 0.

Remember to divide totals by the number of servings.

Son-of-a-Gun in a Sack

Servings: Makes one loaf. Serves twelve.

This interesting recipe is similar to steamed pudding and Christmas pudding. It is a Historic Ranch and Trail Drive Recipe from the *Cowboy Cookbook,* by the Society for Range Management. The English plum pudding must surely have been its original inspiration. Their background information states that when the ranch cook wanted to be especially nice to the cowhands, he made a boiled pudding sometimes called Son-of-a-Gun in a Sack. Raisins or dried apples and suet were added to a soft dough. Following the old colonial method, the mass was placed in a cloth sack and boiled in a big kettle of water until done. Perhaps it got its name because it was so much trouble to make.

Ingredients	All-Dry
2 cups enriched flour	2 cups
1½ cups soft bread crumbs	1½ cups croutons
½ cup packed brown sugar	½ cup
1 tablespoon baking soda	1 tablespoon
1 teaspoon cinnamon	1 teaspoon
¼ teaspoon ground cloves	¼ teaspoon
¼ teaspoon ground nutmeg	¼ teaspoon
1 cup packed seedless raisins	1 cup
1 cup raw beef suet	1 cup shortening powder
½ cup chopped dried pecans	½ cup
⅔ cup canned evaporated whole milk	⅓ cup powder
½ cup light cane molasses	⅓ cup powder
nil water	2⅓ cups

Instructions: In a mixing bowl combine flour, breadcrumbs, sugar, soda, salt, cinnamon, cloves, and nutmeg. Stir in raisins, suet, and nuts. Stir in milk and molasses, mix well. Arrange layers of cheesecloth to form a sixteen-inch square about one-eighth-inch thick; set in a one-quart bowl. Fill cheesecloth with pudding mix ture; bring up sides of cheesecloth, allowing room for expansion of the pudding. Tie tightly with string. Place the "sack" in a colander. Put colander in kettle and add enough boiling water to cover the sack. Cover, and boil gently for two hours. Remove colander from pan and remove cheesecloth from around pudding at once. Turn pudding, round side up, onto a plate. Let stand for thirty minutes before serving. Serve warm with whipped cream, if desired.

(RECIPE COURTESY OF THE SOCIETY FOR RANGE MANAGEMENT)

Recipe Totals: 4,965 calories, 601 g carbohydrates (20 g dietary fiber and 356 g sugars), 206 mg cholesterol, 272 g total fat (131 g saturated fat), 56 g protein, 4,407 mg sodium.
Dietary Exchanges (recipe totals): Bread, 13.6; Fat, 52.4; Fruit, 15.5; Lean Meat, 0.551; Milk, 1.33; Vegetables, 0.
Remember to divide totals by the number of servings.

Peanutty Chocolate Chip Bars

Servings: Makes three dozen bars. Serves eighteen.

These are great snack bars to take or make on a trip. They are faintly reminiscent of peanut butter cups.

Ingredients	All-Dry
3 cups pudding-type, dry yellow cake mix	3 cups
2 raw whole eggs, extra-large	4 tablespoons whole egg powder
1 cup chunky peanut butter	1 cup powdered peanuts
6 ounces semisweet chocolate chips	1 cup
⅔ cup whole milk	¼ cup powder
nil water	1¾ cups
nil butter powder	½ cup

Instructions: Combine all ingredients. Mix well. Pour into a greased, floured pan and bake at 350 degrees F for twenty minutes. Let cool before cutting—if you can wait.

Recipe Totals: 4,768 calories, 585 g carbohydrates (33 g dietary fiber and 481 g sugars), 513 mg cholesterol, 245 g total fat (74 g saturated fat), 109 g protein, 5,033 mg sodium.
Dietary Exchanges (recipe totals): Bread, 9.77; Fat, 37.7; Fruit, 28; Lean Meat, 10.2; Milk, 0.581; Vegetables, 0.
Remember to divide totals by the number of servings.

Stuffed Apples

Servings: Makes four servings.

I think a baked apple, well prepared, is just about one of the best desserts around. If you're not restricted by weight and space, take lots of apples with you and get creative. Maybe a few caramels dropped into the center of the apple before baking would be a good start. If you don't want to use wine, use water or grape juice.

Ingredients	All-Dry
¼ cup packed golden seedless raisins	¼ cup
½ cup red wine	¼ cup powder
¼ cup chopped dried English walnuts	¼ cup
2 tablespoons white granulated sugar	2 tablespoons
½ teaspoon grated fresh orange peel	¼ teaspoon dried
½ teaspoon cinnamon	½ teaspoon
4 large apples with peel	2 cups low-moisture dried apple
1 tablespoon butter	1 tablespoon shortening powder
1½ cups water	3½ cups

Instructions: Soak raisins in wine. Combine raisins (drained), nuts, sugar, orange rind, and cinnamon. Set aside. Core the apples, but do not cut through the bottoms. Take a pie tin and set it on a large piece of aluminum foil. Put the apples on the pie tin, fill each center with one-quarter of the orange mixture and one-quarter of the butter. Bring foil up over apples and seal all edges well. Place cooking rack and water in a six-quart pressure cooker. Place sealed pie tin with apples on the rack and place pressure regulator on the vent pipe. Cook for ten minutes at fifteen pounds pressure. Cool at once. Serve hot or cold.

Note: The instructions have been changed to facilitate out-of-home cooking. Also, if you are preparing the all-dry recipe, use a greased loaf pan or bowl, and put apples and two cups water in first. Mix all other ingredients and put on top of the apple mixture. Bake as above, but reduce the cooking time to five minutes.

(FROM A RECIPE BY NATIONAL PRESTO IND.)

(see next page for recipe nutritional data)

Recipe Totals: 1,104 calories, 196 g carbohydrates (20 g dietary fiber and 161 g
sugars), 31 mg cholesterol, 33 g total fat (9 g saturated fat), 8 g protein,
132 mg sodium.
Dietary Exchanges (recipe totals): Bread, 0.3; Fat, 3.93; Fruit, 13; Lean Meat, 0;
Milk, 0; Vegetables, 0.
Remember to divide totals by the number of servings.

Quick Fruit Cobbler

Servings: Makes six to eight servings.

I have made this recipe so very many times. It's always a big hit. You can use
any fruit you want—they all work equally well for a quick cobbler.

Ingredients	All-Dry
4 cups fresh peeled apple slices	2 cups dried apples
¾ cup white granulated sugar	¾ cup
1 teaspoon cinnamon	1 teaspoon
1⅓ cups biscuit mix	1⅓ cups
½ cup whole milk	⅙ cup powder
1 raw whole egg, extra-large	2 tablespoons powder
3 tablespoons Touch of Butter spread	3 tablespoons powdered butter
nil water	2¾ cups

Instructions: Combine fruit, sugar, and cinnamon, and put in a
deep buttered pan. Mix all other ingredients and spoon over the
top. Bake for twenty minutes at 375 degrees F.

*Note: If you're using all-dry ingredients, add two-and-a-half cups
boiling water to apples (water quantity may vary with different dried
fruit) and let steep for ten minutes or until cool. Continue mixing
according to the recipe, including liquid.*

Recipe Totals: 2,197 calories, 362 g carbohydrates (10 g dietary fiber and 211 g
sugars), 267 mg cholesterol, 75 g total fat (21 g saturated fat), 31 g protein, 3,305
mg sodium.
Dietary Exchanges (recipe totals): Bread, 0; Fat, 2.18; Fruit, 13.2; Lean Meat, 1.1;
Milk, 0.5; Vegetables, 0.
Remember to divide totals by the number of servings.

Williamsburg Queen's Cake

Servings: Makes one loaf. Serves eight.

This cake has such a wonderful flavor that you won't have to worry about what to do with the leftovers. While it calls for currants, I like it with golden raisins instead—it's heavenly.

Ingredients	All-Dry
1 cup unsalted butter	¾ cup powder
1 cup white granulated sugar	1 cup
5 raw whole eggs, extra-large	10 tablespoons powder
1 teaspoon natural lemon flavoring	1 teaspoon
2 cups plus 1 tablespoon enriched flour	2 cups plus 1 tablespoon
½ teaspoon double-acting baking powder	½ teaspoon
½ teaspoon cinnamon	½ teaspoon
2 cups dried currants	2 cups
nil water	1⅓ cups

Instructions: Preheat oven to 325 degrees F. Cream butter and sugar. Add eggs and beat well. Add all other ingredients and blend. Pour into a parchment-lined loaf pan. Reduce oven temperature to 300 degrees F and bake cake for an hour and twenty minutes.

Recipe Totals: 4,607 calories, 625 g carbohydrates (29 g dietary fiber and 406 g sugars), 1,732 mg cholesterol, 216 g total fat (124 g saturated fat), 76 g protein, 668 mg sodium.

Dietary Exchanges (recipe totals): Bread, 11.8; Fat, 50.8; Fruit, 25; Lean Meat, 5.52; Milk, 0; Vegetables, 0.

Remember to divide totals by the number of servings.

APPENDIX A

About Flour

Not all grains contain gluten, the elastic material that allows a yeast bread to rise. Usually, the amount of protein in a grain determines the amount of gluten it contains, and that, in turn, determines the amount of tolerance a dough has, or how much it can be manipulated before the gluten breaks down. Here are the major characteristics of the grains and blends of grain most commonly available to us:

PROPERTIES OF COMMON GRAINS

Amaranth: High in protein, but low in gluten, amaranth is not a good flour for yeast breads by itself, but is good when blended with wheat.

Barley: Malted barley flour, which is made from sprouted whole grain, is mixed with wheat flour as a yeast food.

Buckwheat: Not really a grain—it is high in fat.

Corn: Sometimes called Indian meal, cornmeal is not a high-gluten meal.

Cornell Formula: For people sensitive to wheat bran. To make your own, take one cup of unbleached all-purpose flour. Remove two tablespoons and one teaspoon of flour, and replace them with one tablespoon of powdered milk, one tablespoon of soy flour, and one teaspoon of wheat germ. Use the resulting blend as you would use whole-wheat flour.

Millet: A very high-protein grain. Can be substituted in equal amounts for wheat.

Oats: Oats are high in protein but produce no gluten.

Rice: Good as a thickening agent, or for people with wheat intolerance. Usually blended with other flours.

(text continued on page 143)

FLOUR—WHAT'S IN IT FOR YOU

Weight and Nutritional Value of One Cupful of Flour

Type of Flour:	grams	cal	protein (g)	carb. (g)	fat (g)	fiber (g)	vit.A (IU)	thiamin (mg)
K.A. unbleached all-purpose flour	115	400	13.0	87.0	2.0	3.0	0	.80
K.A. whole-wheat flour	120	400	16.0	85.2	2.4	11.5	0	.66
Wheat germ (toasted)	112	400	36.0	48.0	12.0	13.2	0	1.88
Wheat bran (raw)	57	120	13.0	36.0	2.6	26.0	n/a	.42
Amaranth (grain)	195	729	28.2	129.0	12.7	7.4	0	.16
Barley (pearled)	200	698	16.4	157.6	2.0	1.0	0	.24
Barley (Scotch)	200	696	19.2	154.4	2.2	1.8	0	.42
Buckwheat (light)	98	340	6.3	77.9	1.2	.5	0	.08
Buckwheat (dark)	98	326	11.5	70.6	2.5	1.6	0	.57
Cornmeal (whole, yellow)	122	433	11.2	89.9	4.8	2.0	620	.46
Cornmeal (whole, white)	122	433	11.2	89.9	4.8	2.0	0	.46
Millet (unground)	200	756	22.0	146.0	8.4	17.0	n/a	.84
Oatmeal	80	312	11.4	54.6	5.9	n/a	0	.48
Rice flour	113	398	7.1	91.0	.9	n/a	0	.52
Rye (medium)	111	400	12.2	81.0	2.2	n/a	0	.33
Rye (whole-grain flour)	128	419	20.9	87.2	3.3	3.1	0	.78
Soy (full fat)	85	360	32.0	27.1	17.3	1.4	102	.49
Triticale flour	130	440	17.1	95.1	2.4	2.0	0	.49

141

Type of Flour	grams	riboflavin (mg)	niacin (mg)	sodium (mg)	calcium (mg)	potassium (mg)	phosphorus (mg)	iron (mg)
K.A. unbleached all-purpose flour	115	.34	6.2	2	22	130	112	5.00
K.A. whole-wheat flour	120	.14	5.2	9	49	444	446	4.00
Wheat germ (toasted)	112	.92	6.4	4	52	1072	1300	7.20
Wheat bran (raw)	57	.20	12.0	0	60	636	920	8.28
Amaranth (grain)	195	.41	2.5	42	298	714	887	14.81
Barley (pearled)	200	.10	6.2	6	32	320	378	4.00
Barley (Scotch)	200	.14	7.4	n/a	68	592	580	5.40
Buckwheat (light)	98	.04	.4	n/a	11	314	86	1.00
Buckwheat (dark)	98	.15	2.8	n/a	32	490	340	2.70
Cornmeal (whole, yellow)	122	.13	2.4	1	24	346	312	2.90
Cornmeal (whole, white)	122	.13	2.4	1	24	346	312	2.90
Millet (unground)	200	.58	9.4	n/a	16	390	568	6.00
Oatmeal	80	.11	2.6	2	42	282	324	3.60
Rice flour	113	.59	2.9	45	13	168	249	3.28
Rye (medium)	111	.11	1.3	5	22	322	152	2.78
Rye (whole-grain flour)	128	.28	3.5	1	69	1101	686	5.80
Soy (full fat)	85	.99	3.7	11	175	2138	420	5.42
Triticale flour	130	.17	3.7	3	45	805	417	3.37

Note: All charts and information in this appendix are reprinted with the permission of Ms. Brinna Sands, vice-president of the King Arthur Flour Company and author of the *King Arthur Flour 200th Anniversary Cookbook*.

Rye: Contains more minerals than wheat, but is low in gluten. Rye must be combined with wheat for yeast bread.

Soy flour: A tremendous source of complete protein—almost forty percent—which puts it on the same level as meat, fish, or poultry. Usually blended with other flours.

Triticale: A cross between wheat and rye, it lacks gluten and must be blended for yeast breads. It is high in protein and has a more balanced amino-acid profile.

Facts About Dairy Products

Cows' milk: Milk consists of 87 percent water, 3.5 percent fat, 3.5 percent protein, 4.9 percent lactose (milk sugar) and 0.7 percent minerals. Thirty percent of milk's calories come from fat.

Buttermilk: Modern buttermilk is made from a culture, much the same as yogurt. Even fat-free buttermilk is a creamy product.

Cream: It has many of the nutrients of milk, but with a concentrated portion of fat.

Cream cheese: It is lower in protein and calcium than other cheeses. Ninety percent of cream cheese's calories come from fat.

Cottage cheese: Made from just the protein of milk, it is low in calcium but is also lower in fat than most cheese.

Clotted cream: Cream that is scooped off and refrigerated after the milk has been allowed to ripen at room temperature for a day-and-a-half.

Condensed milk: Whole milk with the water removed and sugar added. One can of condensed milk equals two-and-a-half cups of milk and half a cup of sugar.

Eggs: The protein in eggs is complete and can complement the partial protein in grains. Eggs are very nutritious. More than half of an egg's fat is unsaturated.

Evaporated milk: Milk with more than half of the water removed by evaporation. It makes a good substitute for cream.

Sour cream: A high-fat version of buttermilk and yogurt.

Sour milk: To make sour milk from pasteurized milk, blend one tablespoon vinegar or lemon juice with one cup of regular milk. Let stand for five minutes to curdle.

Yogurt: Made from a bacterial culture introduced to pasteurized milk. The bacteria are similar to those in the human digestive tract so yogurt is digested easily.

✳ APPENDIX C ✳
All About Fats

America's ongoing love-hate relationship with fat probably wins it more press coverage than is given to any other nutrient. We need fat to carry fat-soluble vitamins around our bodies; we also need it to store the fuel we burn. Fat stores energy much more efficiently than carbohydrates or protein do; one gram of fat will produce nine calories of energy, compared with only four calories each from the other two. For good health, we need to eat all types of fat. Since fat makes things taste good, it is sometimes difficult to eat as little as we need. If we bear in mind that about thirty percent of our calories should come from fat, that tells us when we should quit eating it. And if we are eating as many complex carbohydrates as we should, quitting will be easier.

CHOLESTEROL

Cholesterol is an unsaturated, solid alcohol that feels and looks like a soft, greasy soap. It is found in the fatty tissues of animals. Our bodies manufacture cholesterol—about a gram a day—since it is necessary for building the membranes of our body cells and other membranes that surround our nerves. Cholesterol also produces the hormones that determine our gender.

There seems to be a connection between too much cholesterol and heart disease. Excess cholesterol can accumulate in, and clog, our arteries, creating stress on the whole circulatory system. Whether what we eat contributes to the accumulation of cholesterol in our bodies and, ultimately, heart disease, is still not certain. Some people seem to be able to eat anything they want; others are apparently much more vulnerable.

In general, it seems wise to keep your level of cholesterol below the magic number of 200. This means 200 milligrams of cholesterol per deciliter of blood. A deciliter is one-tenth of a liter, or a bit less than one cup. We are told we can help achieve this goal by carefully choosing the fats we eat.

Types of Fat

Fats can be divided into three groups: saturated, monounsaturated, and polyunsaturated. Saturated fats apparently help create cholesterol. Monounsaturated fats seem to have no effect on cholesterol levels. Polyunsaturated fats help cholesterol pass through the system.

Interestingly, eating foods that contain cholesterol does not have as much effect on our own blood cholesterol levels as eating foods high in saturated fats.

Of the 600 "fat" calories we may eat daily in an average 2,000-calorie diet, a good balance is one-third saturated fat, one-third mono-unsaturated fat, and one-third polyunsaturated fat. This minimizes the bad effects of any one type and helps maximize its positive aspect.

The following chart analyzes various fats. Note that vegetable oils and shortenings contain no nutrition other than fat. Olive oil contains a small amount of iron. A tablespoon of butter or margarine contains about 470 international units (IU) of vitamin A, making them the only fats other than cheese to contain any significant nutrition, apart from calories.

Incidentally, when we speak of food containing a certain number of calories, we really mean its potential to produce a certain amount of energy. One calorie is the amount of energy required to raise the temperature of one kilogram of water (a bit more than a quart) one degree centigrade (1.8 degrees Fahrenheit) at one atmosphere of pressure—in other words, average pressure at sea level.

Fats: The Hard Facts

Fat	% saturated	% mono-unsat.	% poly-unsat.
safflower oil	9	13	78
sunflower oil	11	21	68
corn oil	13	25	62
sesame oil	14	42	44
olive oil	14	77	9
peanut oil	18	48	34
soy lecithin	15	40	49
margarine	19	53	28
shortening (veg.)	25	68	7
cottonseed oil	27	18	55
lard	41	43	16
palm oil	53	38	9
butter	68	28	4
coconut oil	92	6	2

Characteristics of Cooking Fats

Butter: Butter is only 80 percent fat. The remainder is water and milk solids. It is available either with or without salt (sweet butter). The salted variety will keep longer. The unsalted variety has a delicious and delicate flavor.

Butter and vegetable-oil blends: These blends are a great compromise between flavor and nutrition. There are several varieties on the market, providing different ratios of saturated and unsaturated fats. Most can be used where butter is called for in a recipe. They cannot be used in puff pastry or puff dough.

Cheese: Cheese is made from the curd (protein) in milk, in combination with fat. Hard cheeses like Cheddar, Romano, Parmesan, Swiss, etc., are very concentrated, containing up to 80 percent fat. That is more than well-marbled beef, which is only 50 to 60 percent fat. When using them, think of them as you would meat and eat an equivalent amount. Nutritionally, cheese has the same values as milk with lots of high-quality protein, calcium, and vitamins A and D. Processed cheese is usually lower in fat than "real" cheese but often contains more salt.

Clarified butter: This is a pure butter that is all fat. Butter, remember, is only 80 percent fat. To make it, melt the butter, boil off the water, chill the remainder and remove the non-fat solids which will have settled on the bottom.

Lard: This is an animal fat rendered from pork. It is softer and oilier than other solid fats. Because of its large crystalline structure, it works well in biscuits and is unsurpassed for pie crusts, but won't create as fine a grain in cakes. As you can see from the table above, lard is not on the bottom of the list nutritionally. If you use butter in baking (and as long as you're not a vegetarian), you can certainly feel comfortable with lard.

Margarine: This is a vegetable-oil version of butter and, like butter, contains 80 percent fat. It is fortified with vitamin A. The oils have been hydrogenated to make them solid at room temperature. Some of them contain more saturated fat than others, so if that is what you are trying to avoid, check the labels.

Shortening: This term initially included all fats and oils. It refers to the ability of fat to break up and weaken the gluten connections in flour, or to "shorten" them. That's what makes cakes, cookies, and pie crusts, tender. Today, this term is generally used for vegetable shortening, a vegetable-oil equivalent of lard that also has been hydrogenated to make it solid at room temperature.

Vegetable shortening contains no cholesterol and, depending on the oils used, less saturated fat. Check your labels to be sure of what you're getting. It's used very much as lard is, but is stable at room temperature, so it will keep almost indefinitely. For this reason, it is the basis of many mixes. It can also replace butter when the flavor of butter is not important.

Reprinted with permission of Brinna Sands, vice-president of King Arthur Flour Company and author of *King Arthur Flour 200th Anniversary Cookbook.*

APPENDIX D
Sweeteners

Sweeteners, like fat, tenderize a dough. They are also hygroscopic, which means they absorb moisture readily. Sweeteners also help keep the final product fresh longer.

CHARACTERISTICS OF SWEETENERS

Brown sugar: A combination of granular sugar and molasses. To make your own, mix a quarter-cup of molasses with each cup of granulated sugar.

Cinnamon sugar: This is a combination of granulated sugar and a tablespoon or two of cinnamon powder per cup.

Citrus sugar: A flavored sugar with two to three teaspoons of lemon or orange zest (the grated outer rind) per cup of granular sugar.

Confectioner's sugar, or powdered sugar: This is sugar that has been ground to a powder. Cornstarch is added to keep it dry and stop it from forming lumps.

Granulated sugar: The most common sugar used today. The only sweetener better than granular sugar is blackstrap molasses.

Honey: A natural sweetener made by honeybees. Do not bake with honey at temperatures over 400 degrees F, or the honey might scorch. Lower the temperature twenty-five degrees and cook for five or ten minutes longer.

Icing sugar: Very fine, granular sugar, sometimes called castor sugar.

Liquid sweeteners: Sweeteners such as honey and molasses allow you to reduce the liquid in a recipe. Molasses is 24 percent water, which means you can reduce the water in your recipe by a quarter-cup for each cup of molasses you substitute for granulated sugar.

Maple syrup: It takes between thirty-five and fifty gallons of maple sap to make one gallon of maple syrup.

Molasses: A byproduct of the sugar-refining process. It is a major constituent of bagasse, the residue left after pure sugar is extracted from sugar cane.

Turbinado sugar: A cleaned-up variety of raw sugar. It can be sold in the United States when the harmful impurities have been removed. Real raw sugar is an illegal import.

Vanilla sugar: A flavored sugar made by packing sugar with vanilla beans for two weeks before use, so the sugar can absorb some of the bean's volatile oil.

Reprinted with permission of Brinna Sands, vice-president of King Arthur Flour Company and author of *King Arthur Flour 200th Anniversary Cookbook.*

* Appendix E *
Gluten Intolerance

Some people develop an allergic reaction to gluten and must eliminate it from their diet. One of my friends and sales representatives, Joan Siska, of Alberta, Canada, has a daughter with gluten intolerance. It makes buying bread and many other items impossible. Joan has a special substitute for wheat flour in quick breads. Her recipe makes three cups of flour:

2 cups white rice flour
⅔ cup potato starch (you cannot substitute potato flour)
⅓ cup tapioca flour
1 extra egg or egg white

Joan said you don't have to increase the water in the recipe with this blend. You will have a stiff dough, about like a biscuit dough. When you use this mixture for the first time as a cup-for-cup exchange in a new recipe, add your liquid gradually to acquire the right consistency. If the dough appears stiffer than it should be, add water a tablespoonful at a time until it is moist enough, and the dough is of the right consistency. Then mark your recipe accordingly.

According to Joan, this recipe exchange will work with yeast if you add a teaspoon of vinegar. Joan and her husband, Ralph, say they also use equal parts of rice flour, potato starch, and tapioca flour, along with one or two extra egg whites, to make yeast bread in their bread machine.

Other gluten-free yeast bread recipes use xanthan gum, unflavored gelatin, and guar gum to make the dough pliable and prevent crumbling. About one to three tablespoons of these ingredients is the amount usually needed.

Flours made from beans, peas, and nuts are another gluten-free possibility, usually as one-fourth of the bulk mixture. Cornstarch, another good product, will give a smoother-textured bread, and complement the protein of these products.

I hope you find these suggestions helpful. I'd love to hear from any of you regarding your own successful blends, if you're willing to share them. You can reach me at: Adventure Foods, 481 Banjo Lane, Whittier, NC 28789.

Cooking Measurements

COMMON EQUIVALENTS

Teaspoon(s) (tsp)

dash	= less than ⅛ tsp
1 tsp	= ⅓ tablespoon or 5 milliliters (ml)
1½ tsp	= ½ tablespoon
3 tsp	= 1 tablespoon or 15 ml
8 tsp	= 1 ounce

Tablespoon(s) (Tbs or Tbsp)

1 Tbs	= 3 tsp
2 Tbs	= ⅛ cup or 1 fluid ounce
4 Tbs	= ¼ cup
5⅓ Tbs	= ⅓ cup
8 Tbs	= ½ cup or ¼ pint
10⅔ Tbs	= ⅔ cup
12 Tbs	= ¾ cup
14 Tbs	= ⅞ cup
16 Tbs	= 1 cup

Cups (C)

⅜ cup	= 6 Tbs
⅓ cup	= 5 Tbs plus 1 tsp
½ cup	= 1 tea cup
1 cup	= 240 ml or ½ pint
2 cups	= 16 fluid ounces or 1 pint
4 cups	= 1 quart

Volume of Dry and Solid Food

1 square of chocolate	= 4 Tbs
1 cup	= ½ pint
juice of one lemon	= 3 Tbs
3 medium carrots	= 1 cup
2 stalks celery	= 1 cup
1 medium pepper	= 1 cup
8 egg whites	= 1 cup
12 egg yolks	= 1 cup
4 quarts	= 1 gallon
2 gallons	= 1 peck
4 pecks	= 1 bushel
16 ounces (dry)	= 1 pound
1 stick butter	= ¼ pound or ½ cup
2 large eggs or 3 medium eggs	= ½ cup

Liquid Measurements

1 tsp	= ⅙ ounce
1½ tsp	= ½ Tbs
3 tsp	= 1 Tbs (15 ml)
1 Tbs	= ½ ounce or 15 grams
1 jigger	= 1½ fluid ounces
2 Tbs	= ⅛ cup (30 ml) or one fluid ounce
4 Tbs	= ¼ cup (60 ml) or 2 fluid ounces
8 Tbs	= ½ cup (120 ml) or 4 fluid ounces
16 Tbs	= 1 cup or 8 fluid ounces (240 ml) or 227 grams
2 cups	= 1 pint or 16 fluid ounces
2 pints or 4 cups	= 1 quart or 32 fluid ounces (slightly less than 1 liter)
2 quarts	= ½ gallon or 64 fluid ounces
1 gallon	= 128 fluid ounces or 16 cups

Ounce Equivalents

1 square of chocolate	= 1 ounce
2 Tbs sugar	= 1 ounce
3 ½ Tbs baking powder	= 1 ounce
4 Tbs flour	= 1 ounce
4 Tbs butter	= 1 ounce
4 Tbs cinnamon	= 1 ounce
1 medium egg	= 2 ounces
1 cup bread crumbs	= 3½ ounces
1 cup unsifted cake flour	= 3⅞ ounces
1 cup unsifted flour	= 4¼ ounces
1 cup cornstarch	= 4½ ounces
1 cup powdered sugar	= 4¾ ounces
1 cup granular sugar	= 7 ounces
1 cup honey	= 12 ounces

Reprinted with permission, *The BakePacker's Companion.*

Equivalent Substitutions

The items below are listed in alphabetical order so that you may quickly scan to what you need and find a substitute for it. All items are listed twice, so you only need to scan the second column.

1 cup	apple juice	=	1 ounce apple-juice powder plus 8 ounces water
2 tsp	arrowroot	=	2 Tbs flour
½ tsp	baking powder	=	1 egg white
2 tsp	baking powder	=	½ tsp baking soda
1 tsp	baking powder	=	¼ tsp baking soda plus ½ tsp cream of tartar
½ tsp	baking soda	=	2 tsp baking powder
½ tsp	cream of tartar	=	1 tsp baking powder
1 Tbs	bouillon	=	1 bouillon cube
1	bouillon cube	=	1 Tbs bouillon
1	bouillon cube	=	1 Tbs gravy powder
1⅔ cups	bread crumbs	=	1 cup all-purpose flour
¾ ounce	bread crumbs	=	1 ounce flour
1 cup	butter	=	1 cup lard or shortening
1 cup	butter	=	⅞ cup vegetable oil
1 cup	butter	=	½ cup suet
1 cup	buttermilk	=	1 cup yogurt
3 Tbs	carob, plus 2 Tbs milk or water	=	1 ounce chocolate
4 Tbs	carob, plus 1 Tbs fat	=	1 ounce chocolate

1 ounce	chocolate	=	3 Tbs carob plus 2 Tbs milk or water
1 ounce	chocolate	=	4 Tbs carob plus 1 Tbs fat
1 cup less 2 Tbs	cornmeal	=	1 cup all-purpose flour
1½ cups	corn syrup	=	1 cup sugar (but reduce liquid in recipe by ½ cup)
⅔ ounce	cornstarch	=	1 ounce flour
1 Tbs	cornstarch	=	2 Tbs flour
1 cup	cream	=	1 cup evaporated milk
1 cup	cream, heavy	=	⅗ cup milk plus ⅔ cup fat
1 cup	cream, sour	=	1 cup evaporated milk plus 1 Tbs vinegar
2 cups	cream, whipped	=	1 cup instant dry milk, plus 1 cup iced water beaten with ¼ cup lemon juice and ½ cup sugar
1	egg	=	2 Tbs powdered egg plus 2 Tbs water
1 cup	egg whites	=	8 large eggs or 10 medium-to-small eggs
1	egg white	=	½ tsp baking powder
1	egg, whole	=	2 egg yolks, plus 1 Tbs water
2 Tbs	egg, powdered, plus 2 Tbs water	=	1 egg
1 cup	egg yolks	=	12 large eggs or 14 medium- to-small eggs
12 large, or 14 medium, or 14 small	eggs	=	1 cup egg yolks
8 large, or 10 medium, or 10 small	eggs	=	1 cup egg whites
2	egg yolks, plus 1 Tbs water	=	1 whole egg
7	egg yolks	=	1 ounce flour
2 Tbs	flour	=	2 tsp arrowroot
1 ounce	flour	=	¾ ounce bread crumbs

EQUIVALENT SUBSTITUTIONS

1 ounce	flour	=	⅔ ounce cornstarch
2 Tbs	flour	=	1 Tbs cornstarch
1 ounce	flour	=	7 egg yolks
1 ounce	flour	=	1⅓ ounces minute tapioca
1 cup	all-purpose flour	=	1⅔ cup bread crumbs
1 cup	all-purpose flour	=	1 cup, less 2 Tbs, cornmeal
1 cup	all-purpose flour	=	l cup graham, oat, or rye flour
1 cup less 2 Tbs	bread flour, white or wheat	=	1 cup pastry flour
1 cup	flour, graham, oat, or rye	=	1 cup all-purpose flour
1 cup	flour, pastry	=	1 cup white or wheat bread flour, less 2 Tbs
½ cup	fruit, dried	=	one fresh medium-sized fruit
1 fresh	fruit, medium	=	½ cup dried fruit
1 clove	garlic	=	⅛ tsp garlic powder
⅛ tsp	garlic powder	=	1 clove of garlic
1 Tbs	gravy powder	=	1 bouillon cube
½ tsp	herbs, dried	=	1 Tbs fresh herbs
1 Tbs	herbs, fresh	=	½ tsp dried herbs
1 cup	honey	=	1¼ cups granulated sugar plus ¼ cup water
⅔ cup	honey	=	1 cup sugar
1 cup	lard or shortening	=	1 cup butter
3½ Tbs	lemon juice	=	juice of 1 lemon
⅔ cup	maple syrup	=	1 cup sugar
1 cup	milk	=	½ cup evaporated milk plus ½ cup water
1 cup	milk	=	¼ cup dried whole milk plus 1 cup water
1 cup	milk	=	1 cup reconstituted non-fat dried milk plus 2 tsp margarine

1 cup	milk, plus 1 Tbs lemon or vinegar	=	1 cup sour milk
¼ cup	milk, dried, whole, plus 1 cupwater	=	1 cup fresh milk
1 cup	milk, evaporated	=	3 cups fresh milk, when whipped
½ cup	milk, evaporated, plus ½ cup water	=	1 cup fresh milk
1 cup	milk, evaporated	=	1 cup cream
⅔ cup	milk, plus ⅔ cup fat	=	1 cup heavy cream
1 cup	milk, evaporated, plus 1 Tbs vinegar	=	1 cup sour cream
1 cup	milk, instant dry, plus 1 cup iced water beaten with ¼ cup lemon juice and ½cup sugar	=	2 cups whipped cream
1 cup	milk, non-fat, dry reconstituted, plus 2 tsp margarine	=	1 cup milk
4 Tbs	milk, non-fat dry, plus 1 cupwater	=	1 cup skim milk
1 cup	milk, skim	=	1 cup water plus 4 Tbs non-fat dry milk
1 cup	milk, sour	=	1 cup milk plus 1 Tbs lemon or vinegar
1 cup	molasses	=	1 cup sugar
1 tsp	mustard, Dijon-style	=	1 tsp mustard powder
1 tsp	mustard powder	=	1 tsp Dijon-style mustard
1 tsp	onion powder	=	¼ fresh minced onion
1 tsp	onion, minced, dried	=	¼ fresh minced onion
¼	onion, minced, fresh	=	1 tsp onion powder
1 fresh	pepper	=	⅓ cup sweet pepper flakes
⅓ cup	pepper, sweet flakes	=	1 fresh pepper

½ cup	suet	=	1 cup butter
1 cup	sugar	=	1⅓ cups firmly packed brown sugar
1 cup	sugar	=	1½ cups confectioner's sugar
1 cup	sugar	=	1½ cups corn syrup (but reduce liquid in recipe by ½ cup)
1 cup	sugar	=	⅔ cup honey
1 cup	sugar	=	⅔ cup maple syrup
1 cup	sugar	=	1 cup molasses
1⅓ cups	sugar, brown, firmly packed	=	1 cup sugar
1½ cups	sugar, confectioner's	=	1 cup sugar
1¼ cups	sugar, granulated, plus ¼ cup water	=	1 cup honey
1⅓ ounces	tapioca, minute	=	1 ounce flour
⅞ cup	vegetable oil	=	1 cup butter
1 cup	yogurt	=	1 cup buttermilk

Sources

Adventure Foods
481 Banjo Lane
Whittier, NC 28789
phone (704) 497-4113
fax (704) 497-7529
e-mail: adfoods@drake.dnet.net
(*BakePackers, Easy Camp Reflector Oven, GSI Aluminum Dutch Ovens, bulk, packaged, baking supplies*)

Banks Fry-Bake Co.
Pamela Banks
P.O. Box 183
Claverack, NY 12513
phone (518) 851-5207
phone (888) 379-2253
(*Banks Fry-Bake Oven, pot grippers*)

B West Outdoor Specialties
2425 N. Huachuca
Tucson, AZ 85745
phone (520) 628-1990
fax (520) 628-3602
e-mail: ranger@azstarnet.com;
http://www.creativemarket-place.com
(*Boma Stainless Stove, oven, pots, Platpotjie Cast Iron Dutch Oven*)

Burns-Milwaukee Sun Oven Co.
Distributed by Real Goods
Catalog

555 Leslie Street
Ukiah, CA 95482
phone (800) 762-7325
(*Sun Solar Oven*)

Cascade Designs
4000 First Avenue S.
Seattle, WA 98134
phone (206) 583-0583
fax (206) 467-9421
e-mail:
graham|kitty706595276@
mcimail.com
http://www.cascade designs.com
(*OutBack Oven and accessories, baking mixes*)

Fox Hill Corporation
13970 E. Hwy 51
Rozet, WY 82727
phone (800) 533-7883
e-mail: foxhill@vcn.com
www.vcn.com/business/foxhill
(*Sportsman Oven, Outfitter Oven*)

Good Gear-BushBaker
P.O. Box 2625
Chapel Hill, NC 27515
phone (800) 988-4889
e-mail: goodgear@aol.com
www.gorp.goodgear/goodgear.
htm
(*BushBaker and accessories*)

G.S.I. Outdoors
1023 S. Pine Road
Spokane, WA 99206
phone (800) 704-4474
fax (800) 732-0474
(*Cast aluminum Dutch ovens*)

King Arthur Flour Co.
P.O. Box 876
Norwich, VT 05055-0876
phone (800) 827-6836
(*Kuhn Rikon Pressure Cookers,
baking accessories, cookware
baking supplies and cookbooks*)

Mark One Outdoor Outlet
w/Coleman Products
627 N. Morton St.
Bloomington, IN 47404
phone (800) 869-9058
fax (800) 869-9053
(*Coleman Collapsible Oven, outdoor accessories*)

Mirro Aluminum Company
1512 Washington Street
Minitowoc, WI 54220
phone (414) 684-4421
(*Aluminum pressure cooker,
bakeware and accessories*)

National Presto Industries
Eau Claire, WI 54701
phone (715) 839-2121
fax (715) 839-2148
(*Aluminum and stainless pressure
cookers, cookbook, accessories*)

Pyromid Outdoor Cooking
Systems
3292 S. Hwy. 97
Redmond, OR 97756
phone (800) 824-4288
fax (541) 923-1004
e-mail: efw3@aol.com
(*Pyromid stove and oven, accessories*)

Rome Industries
1703 W. Detweiler Dr.
Peoria, IL 61615
phone (800) 818-7603
fax (800) 936-ROME
e-mail: romeind@aol.com M
(*Cast-iron pie irons, aluminum
double Dutch cooker, other baking accessories*)

Society for Range Management
Trail Boss Cowboy Cookbook
1839 York Street
Denver, CO 80206
(Cookbook costs $14.95, plus
$2.00 shipping)
phone (303) 355-7070
fax (303) 355-5059
(*Cookbook, Range Society mem-
bership*)

Strike 2 Industries
508 E. Augusta Avenue
Spokane, WA 99207
phone (509) 484-3701
(*standard and ultra BakePackers*)

Index